THE WAY TO CAPE HORN

Trevor David Clifton

ISBN 9781782804215

For Ida

And

With my special thanks to some special people

Table of Contents

About The Author

Hello,

My name is Trevor David Clifton. I was 65 when I set off from Portsmouth (UK), in September 2005, on my own, to sail around Cape Horn in 'Cracklin' Rosie' my 28ft 'Twister'.

Sailing round 'The Horn' and painting pictures in Patagonia, had been a dream for some time: 'The Horn' because it's the 'Sailor's Everest' and Patagonia because the air is clear and colours and shadows are so sharp. As it transpired it was more difficult getting to 'The Horn' than going round it and most of my paintings came out in pastel shades!

I have been happily married to Ida (pronounced Eeda – she's Dutch) since 1965; we have three sons, two daughters-in-law, one daughter-out-law (!) and five grandchildren.

I served for thirty-four years in The Royal Engineers as far east as Hong Kong, west to St Vincent in the West Indies and lots of places in between.

Since leaving the army I have been teaching sailing, examining Yachtmaster candidates and delivering (mostly sailing) boats here and there.

It's all been a lot of fun - so far…

The Way to Cape Horn (and back)

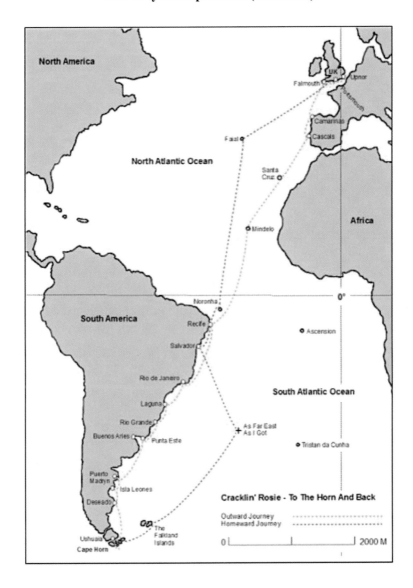

Line Drawing

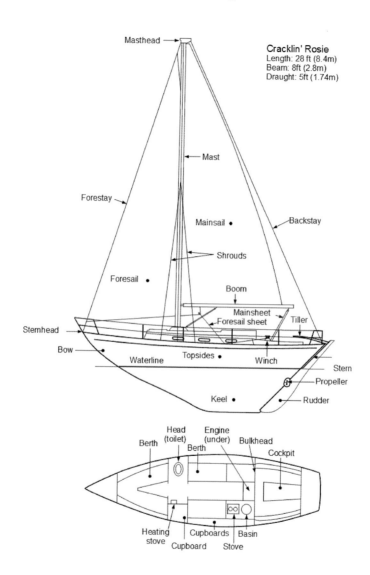

Masthead

Cracklin' Rosie
Length: 28 ft (8.4m)
Beam: 8ft (2.8m)
Draught: 5ft (1.74m)

Mast

Forestay

Mainsail •

Backstay

Shrouds

Foresail •

Boom

Mainsheet
Foresail sheet
Tiller

Stemhead

Bow

Waterline

Topsides •

Winch

Stern

Propeller

Keel •

Rudder

Head (toilet)

Engine (under)

Bulkhead

Berth

Berth

Cockpit

Heating stove

Cupboards

Basin

Cupboard

Stove

Now or Never

The old tractor that we used for towing boats around the hard grumbled into life; Brian, our volunteer harbourmaster, backed it up to Cracklin' Rosie's cradle, I hitched on the heavy, steel-wire towrope; Brian eased in the clutch, the cable tightened and my little boat wobbled and shuddered her way down to the bottom of the slipway where the muddy waters of the River Medway splashed against the concrete.

I waded out through the mud towards the incoming tide, dug in the anchor, tied the end of a long rope onto the ring on the anchor shank and splashed back to the boat, laying out the rope as I went. I scrubbed off my boots, climbed aboard and tied the inboard end of the rope to the cleat on the foredeck while Brian attached a long towrope to the cradle and moved the tractor up above the high-water mark.

I made a cup of tea for both of us then sat in the cockpit to wait.

A soft wind blew in with the tide. The water rose, lapping quietly against the hull. We floated off.

I manhandled Cracklin' Rosie out from her cradle towards the river, unfurled the foresail and left it flapping while I hauled in the anchor.

We drifted upstream with the gently flooding tide; I walked back along the deck, set the foresail and hoisted the main. There was just enough wind to 'ferry-glide' across the stream and clear the end of the pier jutting out from the shore just up-river.

Brian waved as he pulled Cracklin' Rosie's cradle back up the slip to add it to his store of 'things that'll come in useful one day' - I wouldn't be needing it any more.

Slowly we made headway against the incoming current, aiming to pick up a mooring buoy further down the river, but we were in the lee of an ancient brick wall at the river's edge. Every time I made an approach the wind fluttered in the sails and we drifted off.

It took me six attempts before I finally got a line onto the buoy, just as a fellow club member pottered by in a dinghy and congratulated me on my skillful sailing; he hadn't seen the previous five attempts.

Cracklin' Rosie joined our family in 1988 when we lived at Upnor, thirty miles east of London, on the River Medway; I chose her for her good looks, her long keel and relatively heavy displacement. She's an all-GRP 'Twister', a 28 foot sloop.

She lived on the river for ten years, hanging on a buoy beneath the battlements of Upnor Castle; we made trips up the Thames to London, along the south coast and over to the shores of mainland Europe and the Baltic Sea.

Then my other life took over and she sat, quietly mouldering in her cradle on the hard, until the 'now or never' moment arrived.

For years I'd daydreamed about painting pictures in Patagonia and sailing around 'The Horn'; I'd stopped talking about it though after I overheard a friend telling Ida not to worry: "he'll never do it" he'd said. That was a kick up the backside; I'd recently celebrated my sixty-fifth birthday so I thought I'd better get on with it.

I moved back to the Medway Towns and started the re-fit.

Jesse and Kathleen James, old friends from army days, live conveniently nearby; they put me up - and put up with me getting up early, coming home late and falling asleep on the sofa. We did socialise a bit: Kathleen and I discussed the political topics of the day over breakfast. And we were still friends when I finally departed.

Terry and Christine Clothier drove up from their home in Rustington, on the south coast, to help me raise the mast with its shiny, new rigging; Terry helped and Christine directed operations.

I made lots of donations to yacht chandlers, rubbed down her bottom (Cracklin' Rosie's not Christine's) and painted it with 'Coppercoat' - a copper based antifouling with a projected ten-year life span. I sent the echo-sounder to a specialist for servicing, fitted a wind generator, bought new batteries and had the electrics professionally overhauled - after which we did a careful audit of Cracklin' Rosie's power consumption and calculated that the input from the wind-generator, supplemented by an hour's charge from the engine alternator no more than once a day would be enough to keep the lights burning and, more importantly, keep my new electronic steering unit running.

Six weeks of hard work later (Ida says it was longer than that) Cracklin' Rosie was ready to sail, which was a good thing because the engine wouldn't start; I'd already booked it in for an overhaul at

Marine Power in Bursledon on the River Hamble, about a hundred and fifty miles away, a couple of day's sailing or so it should have been.

The river was quiet the evening before I left; the great sheds of Chatham dockyard, where wooden ships were built for the Royal Navy, were silent on the eastern bank of the river; I watched the sun go down over Rochester Cathedral and thought about the adventure ahead.

We sailed with the ebb early in the morning; down the winding river past Garrison Point, leaving the huge bulk of Kingsnorth power station drifting by to port, past Stangate Creek, where sailing ships once rode at anchor waiting for a wind, and out into the River Thames. The cranes and jetties of Sheerness docks slowly faded into the misty horizon astern.

I thought of the times I'd sailed this patch of water before, usually heading for Calais or Boulogne, and once, in a Westerly Centaur, with the spinnaker hoisted sideways because I'd inadvertently attached the guy to the head of the sail and the halyard to one of the clews!

The wind was in the south, perfect for sailing along the north coast of Kent. I headed east along 'Four Fathom Channel' - marked in brackets on the chart as being four fathoms at high water - towards Margate, reaching along comfortably with the wind on the beam; but of course, as we rounded North Foreland the reach turned into a beat, and the tide was against us.

It was dark as I tacked back and forth past Dover. I called Port Control on the radio to let them know what this little boat beating southwards was doing.

"You're OK" came the response, "just stay a mile or so off the entrance and you'll be well clear."

The ferries going in and out of the harbour went by at fifteen knots; they all avoided us.

Street lights along the shore passed by slowly. Navigation lights on the ships making their way down The Channel glimmered in the distance.

The wind was dropping and I dozed in the cockpit for a few minutes at a time. It was a long night. When the sun rose over the horizon the wind was gone; we drifted past Dungeness with the west-going tide.

Making a cup of tea was easy, the only thing that rocked the boat was the wash from passing vessels - and they all passed us, all day.

By the time we got to Beachy Head it was dark again; the beam from the lighthouse flashed on and off, alternately illuminating my limp sails and the white cliffs as we floated slowly past.

The clock had long since chimed midnight when Newhaven's harbour lights came into view. A tiny breeze gave us about a knot through the water; I headed in between the arms of the harbour entrance, desperate to tie up and get some sleep.

We crept forward against the gentle flow of the River Ouse, heading for the marina half a mile upstream. Then the sound of heavy engines rumbled through the night air, soon followed by a cross-channel ferry steaming down the harbour. The wash stopped us dead. The current slowly carried us back out to sea.

Nodding at the helm, I pointed the boat towards the west. Little puffs of wind lifted the sails now and then as we sailed and drifted along the coast.

The morning sun stirred me into action: I called Brighton Marina on the radio and asked if they could accommodate me for a day: friendly staff came out in a launch and towed us in. I tied up to a pontoon, put the batteries on charge and slept.

The wind was about force one from the south-west when I was towed out again in the morning: we made long, slow tacks along the shore; people walking their dogs were overtaking us. For a long time I stared ahead at the big gas holder further along the coast, in Littlehampton, until the white, tent-like feature of the holiday camp in Bognor Regis took its place on the horizon; slowly we passed that too.

Just in the lee of Selsey Bill I anchored close to the shore to sleep and wait for the morning tide.

Cracklin' Rosie tugging gently at her chain woke me up: wind, at last!

I hoisted the mainsail and left it flapping while I hauled in the anchor. We beat out against the southerly wind towards the East

Borough Head buoy, then bore away on a reach through the Looe Channel - which isn't really a channel at all but a route across the shallows which extend out to sea from Selsey Bill.

I must have sailed between the red and green buoys at the western end of the channel at least two dozen times; one is called 'Boulder' and the other 'Street'; I can never remember which one is which.

The beacon outside of the entrance to Chichester Harbour slipped by to starboard, then the Fairway into Langstone Harbour where I had my first little boat at the age of fourteen, fifty years before, blimey!

We sailed through the 'Main Passage' - the gap in the submerged barrier off Southsea beach - and cruised into the familiar waters of The Solent.

Sailing north up the River Hamble with a following wind wasn't going to be difficult but when I called the harbourmaster to let him know my intentions he sent a launch "to make it easier for me" he said; I think he was worried that I might bash into something on the way.

I left Rosie tied up in Bursledon for her engine overhaul.

A week later a healthy sounding Yanmar 12YSE drove us back down the river with my brother-in-law, Billy, at the helm. I'd booked Cracklin' Rosie into Southsea Marina, back in Langstone Harbour and close to home, for the last few days before my departure; Billy had volunteered to help.

We ran out of diesel.

I couldn't believe I'd been so stupid but in the rush of activity before setting off I'd forgotten that the tank was nearly empty and left two cans of fuel at home.

We had a deadline too: the marina is only accessible for a couple of hours either side of high water.

But the wind was fair, we had sails and there wasn't far to go.

Daylight was fading from the autumn afternoon when we reached the fairway leading into the harbour; the evening breeze gave us just enough speed to beat the ebbing tide.

Then that gentle, helpful breeze veered and came in strong from the north; suddenly we were wrestling with the current and I was kicking myself.

In the distance I could see the red and green lights of the two ferry pontoons at the head of the fairway; slowly they grew brighter as we tacked back and forth, making just a few yards on each tack.

The deadline for getting into the marina passed and the wind strength increased. I reefed the mainsail, rolled up the foresail a little and we beat our way further into the dark waters of the harbour.

I rigged fenders and mooring lines and told Billy where to aim the boat. Mooring lines in hand I leapt onto the deserted ferry pontoon as we came alongside and made fast. By now it was three o'clock in the morning so the ferry wasn't running.

Billy's car was in the marina car-park, only a short walk away; we drove home and picked up the two cans of diesel I'd left by the garden gate.

Wind-driven waves were bouncing Cracklin' Rosie against the tyres on the side of the pontoon when we got back.

I poured the diesel into the tank and bled the fuel line. Kneeling on the cabin sole, leaning over the engine as we rocked and rolled was less than comfortable, but it's a simple job and the engine soon burst into life.

We motored down the narrow, winding channel to the 'waiting pontoon' outside of the marina to tie up and sleep for an hour or two, until the tide was high enough for us to get in over the sill.

The next three days passed in a flurry of last bits of maintenance, loading clothes and spares, stowing everything somewhere, somehow, and greeting friends and relatives who came to say 'farewell'.

Meanwhile Ida and our middle son Matt did my shopping. Luke, No1 son and John, No3, were at the back of our house reassembling the sea toilet which I'd decided at the last minute should be overhauled.

I fitted the toilet amidst a shower of goods coming aboard and 'where shall I put this?' questions.

It was late when we went home to bed each evening.

The 'Farewell' moment was to be around mid-day when the tide was high enough for me to get out of the marina.

The pontoon was nearly sinking with the weight of wellwishers who'd come to see me off; Cracklin' Rosie was low in the water too, she was stuffed so full there was barely room to stand anywhere down below.

Matt and John helped me move the boat to the fuel berth for a last top-up with diesel, I kissed most people, shook some hands and cast off.

Portsmouth to Falmouth

We sailed down the fairway towards the open sea; Ida and most of the party were on the beach waving farewell.

Old sailing friends Greg and Sue Hill had brought their lovely ketch, Blue Argolis, around to the marina to join the party, now she was our sailing escort, bedecked with flags and heeling with the weight of people on the side deck waving and shouting last minute good luck messages; she came close alongside to deliver a late 'Bon Voyage' card and kept pace until we were well on the way; then, with a final wave from the crew, she turned back towards the harbour.

I was on my own.

The breeze was southerly and the sea sparkled in the sunshine. My new autohelm steered us westwards, past the old, familiar landmarks: Spit Sand Fort, Cowes, Yarmouth; on through the Hurst Narrows, out past The Needles and across Christchurch Bay towards Studland, where I lowered the anchor in the sheltered bay and spent eighteen hours re-stowing practically everything, toasting our departure and sleeping.

The tall, chalk stacks at the southern end of the bay, known as King Harry Rocks, were sharp against the sky when I hauled in the anchor.

Out past Anvil point we turned towards the west. (Cracklin' Rosie and I had been 'we' for some time now). Sometimes the tide can throw up big waves where it races round the point, but today the sea was kind. Cracklin' Rosie cut through the water under full sail, heading towards the dark bulk of Portland, the rocky peninsular which sticks out five miles into The Channel from the Dorset coast. 'The Race' off Portland Bill is notorious: poems have been written about how stout vessels have foundered in the steep waves which build up when strong winds fight the tide as it rushes around the end of 'The Bill'; however, there are periods in the tidal cycle when, close inshore, there is calm water all the way round the headland, so I slipped into Weymouth to wait for the best time-window and get a few hours' sleep. I cast off again just before midnight.

The breeze was light as I made my approach. I turned on the engine to make sure that we didn't stray into the rougher water; it was still dark but I could see the tumbling, white wave crests ruffling the horizon further out to sea.

We sailed slowly through the day across Lyme Bay; I dozed now and then in the sunshine. When stars began to appear in the darkening sky the lighthouse on Start Point flashed its guiding signal across the waves. We were making about two knots. By midnight we'd passed Prawle Point, the headland at the western end of the bay.

Just before dawn I could see the dark shapes of warships up ahead, there was clearly a naval exercise going on. No announcements or safety warnings came through on the VHF radio so I stuck to the straight line course towards Falmouth. None of the ships ran into us.

The Eddystone light was silhouetted against a beautiful, orange sky as the sun went down; the hills around Plymouth were just visible through the thin haze, ten miles to the north.

The night approach to Falmouth Harbour was easy: visibility was good and the light on St Anthony's Head showed me the way in. There was just a glimmer of morning in the sky when I tied up in a vacant space on a pontoon at Pendennis.

170 Miles 4 Days

Falmouth towards Camarinas, Spain and back To Falmouth

Waves slapping against the hull woke me from a long sleep: the sunshine and gentle winds were gone; flags were flying bar-taut on their halyards. Out in the harbour boats were pitching and rolling on their moorings.

I called home, ticked off a few more jobs from the maintenance list and watched the weather.

Five days later the conditions were right - or so I judged. There was an Atlantic depression tracking north-east across Scotland but the synoptic chart showed well-spaced isobars further south.

I cast off and headed out past Black Rock to the open sea.

The wind was fair, as forecast, but the sea was full of lumps; we dipped the bow into the wave ahead more than a few times.

Out past the Lizard headland the swells rolling in from the Atlantic were a little more regular. With two reefs in the main and a matched foresail we made five knots.

Gannets soared above the waves to entertain me, the miles swished by under the keel and the sunset was beautiful: ragged clouds tinged with red and gold painted on a purple sky; but the wind was rising.

I hoped we were far enough south to miss the worst effects of the depression: we weren't. At 0053 a gale warning for all areas came from Falmouth Coastguard.

By the time we passed latitude 49°N, about fifty miles north-west of Ile d'Oessant – or Ushant as we English speakers call it - the sea was as confused as I'd ever seen it; I looked up at the mast dancing wildly against moonlit clouds racing across the sky. I was pleased (that's putting it mildly) I'd fitted new rigging.

But apart from my dry boat now being rather wet, it was nothing we couldn't handle.

Then there was a loud thump. A big wave crashed into the side of the boat and the cockpit was suddenly full of sea. The sails began to flap wildly as we rounded up towards the wind.

The autohelm was lying on its back, whining.

I grabbed the tiller, bore away a little, and watched the water slowly drain from knee deep to ankle deep, wondering what to do next.

The gale had arrived. I steered by hand for a while, gathering my wits, watching the cockpit empty itself, considering the options. I couldn't steer by hand all the way to Patagonia!

I did have another autohelm, one of the originals, still functioning well but, with eighteen thousand miles to go, carrying on without a spare didn't seem like a good idea.

So what next? Brest? Only fifty miles to the south-east but on a lee shore whose rock strewn approaches might be tricky in rough weather because I didn't have detailed charts of the area.

Heading further south into The Bay of Biscay, graveyard of so many sailing ships, would mean an increasingly western course for NW Spain, against the prevailing winds.

The conclusion I reached fairly quickly was that I needed that autohelm and the best chance of getting it repaired quickly was in the UK.

I turned away from the wind and set the course back towards Falmouth, only a hundred miles away.

Sailing downwind was a delight after the discomfort of beating into such a wild sea; dawn was not far off and the boat was steady enough to make a cup of tea.

I rigged the spare autohelm and ran for home. At least I could enjoy the ride.

Twenty three hours later I tied up in Falmouth Marina and slept until the shops opened. I took the dead machine to 'Sky Wave' the chandlers in Falmouth Marina. We called the manufacturer. "A minimum of ten days" the lady on the end of the phone said, and that was after paying an extra £25 priority-service charge!

I bought a new one.

I called Ida, hired a car and drove back home to Portsmouth. We sat and talked; we hadn't had much time for talking in the rush before I set sail.

Ida told me about her expedition to the supermarket to buy my provisions the day before I left: she'd started by loading the trolley with the thirty-five, two-litre bottles of water I'd put on the shopping list; she stacked the bottles in the car and went back for the next load. Concerned, after loading the third trolley-load, that the car was looking a little low on its springs she called Matt, our middle son, who drove out to help.

In between 'phone calls asking me whether I wanted big onions or small onions and olives in jars or in tins, they'd seen a notice on the shelf where the coffee was displayed offering 'A Free Chocolate Bar With Every Jar'; no-one they asked knew anything about it but by now they'd got to know the girl behind the till, so they wandered back through the aisles to get the details and the free choc bars. The fifth trolley load made the girl laugh: she had to scan in ninety-five tins of baked beans. And, with a bill for over seven-hundred pounds, they were all amused to see the multi-buy savings credit on the receipt: £1.79!

212 Miles 2 Days

Falmouth to Camarinas

Back in Falmouth the weather was looking good so, with Cracklin' Rosie and me full of fuel and provisions, I cast off and headed south again.

'She's a bit low in the water' was a comment I'd heard more than once; but I don't have a water maker and I do have a fear of running dry. Working on a ration of two litres per day for an adult, my seventy-three litre tank, plus a further seventy in containers, should be enough to keep me healthy for seventy days and alive for a bit longer, provided I don't wash; Ida had taken care of that though, with dozens of packets of face-wipes - much more pleasant than splashing cold water on your face in the morning, and you don't have to wash towels.

I spent thirty minutes motoring around in wide circles just outside Falmouth Harbour, calibrating my new autohelm, then watched the Lizard disappear below the horizon astern for the second time that week.

The wind was too strong for full sail so I reefed the main and rolled in about half of the foresail. I could really do with barber-hauling the foresail sheet down to make the sail more efficient when it's rolled like that but it is such a flog, crawling along the lee deck with spray cascading across the coachroof; maybe a snatch block and a pad-eye in the deck, one day.

We passed the point of our previous turn-about, clipped the corner of the separation zone north-west of Ile d'Oessant and carried on southwards for enough miles to put us clear of the tracks of ships sailing between the western end of the English Channel and Cabo Villano on the north-west corner of Spain ('Cape Villain' in English, and aptly named!).

I barely saw another vessel the whole way across The Bay of Biscay until just off the Spanish coast; no dolphins either this trip, too rough for them I expect. We did have a passenger though, a Red Admiral alighted on the chart table and stayed for a while until he decided to take off into the dusk. I watched him fluttering hither and thither in the gusty breeze until I could see him no more; he was heading in the right direction but had about forty miles to go to reach land; I wished him luck.

My planned sleeping programme was difficult to follow at first. I'm not unaccustomed to going without sleep, thirty-four years in the army saw to that, but initially I didn't find sleeping twenty minutes at a time a comfortable routine. I'd chosen the twenty minute period as the length of time it would take from a ship's appearance on the horizon to running me down. Maybe twenty minutes is too long; I have spoken to others who use a fifteen minute period.

Getting comfortable wasn't a problem; I folded one of the cockpit cushion to make a seat, backrest and pillow so that I could just about see all round without lifting my head, although looking astern involved a bit of effort; I could have done with a rear view mirror. Wrapped in foul weather gear, with the collar up and the hood pulled down I was warm and cosy, very cosy; it wasn't long before I found myself waking up, checking the horizon, re-setting the kitchen-timer alarm and going straight back to sleep. But there were no near misses, or even distant ones.

I did see a racing yacht pass across our bows one morning, hull-down and beating to windward; I waved but I don't think they saw me. Looking over your shoulder into the wind and spray when beating is not easy.

Slowly the sea turned to that deep, ocean blue which is beautiful, even when rough; and it did get rough: on day three the pressure fell three millibars in as many hours, a sure sign of a blow; it came with a veer to the east and we raced along with two reefs and a small foresail again.

I began to worry a little about a leak; there was a lot of water in the bilge. I was discharging about ten pump strokes an hour with my 'Whale Gusher10'. I'd searched from stem to stern without finding the source. Lots of areas were wet; tins of beans under the floorboards were paddling if not swimming!

The wind began to ease as we drew nearer to Spain. Just as dawn was breaking about thirty fishing boats appeared out of the darkness in the west; they were strung out in a long line on a slowly converging course. I turned about fifteen degrees to port and gradually overhauled them before turning back towards the coast.

The morning sun rising behind the hills of Galicia was beautiful. I love this part of Spain: green mountains and many, many bays and islands, with friendly little fishing harbours tucked away, unspoiled and waiting to be explored.

We motored across a calm blue sea for the last few hours, past rocky headlands where the Atlantic swells threw up cascades of white water as they crashed into the rocks, and turned in to the little marina by the yacht club in Camarinas.

Jose, the friendly club boatman whom I'd met on a previous visit, waved a welcome and took my lines when I came alongside: "Storm coming" he said.

479 Miles 4½ Days

Camarinas

Camarinas, Spain to Cascais, Portugal

Camarinas is a delightful place to linger for a while, especially after crossing 'The Bay', even more so when the wind is rising.

I lingered. In fact I slept for thirteen hours!

My waking need was easily satisfied: breakfast.

But Cracklin' Rosie needed some love and attention too: I still hadn't found the leak. I improved the anchor chain hawse-pipe plug and re-sealed all the deck fittings. I crawled in through the tiny hatch just aft of the chart table and hung, almost upside down with just my feet sticking out, to check the stern tube flange bolts: with the spanner in my right hand, I supported my weight with my knees and my left hand on the curve of the bilge. The bolts were tight. 'Now' I thought, 'how do I get out of here?' Another thought crossed my mind: 'I could die here and no-one would know for days, probably not until my marina fees were due!' I reached back, pushed the spanner out of the hatch and added the strength of my right arm to the exercise. As I pushed and wriggled backwards and upwards my mobile 'phone slithered out of my pocket, bounced it's way downwards and splashed into the oily water in the bilge; not wishing to venture back into that dark hole again I fished it out with a soup ladle tied to the blunt end of my boathook; but it was dead.

And I still hadn't found the leak.

Then the frying pan was sacrificed. Before I left, Ida had made me promise to fit an automatic bilge pump; the wiring had been installed during the refit, but the pump, still in its plastic wrapping, was in the 'spares cupboard'. Some kind of a mounting was needed: the bilge in a Twister is fairly empty - apart from the water that was leaking into mine. I took a hack-saw, turned the frying pan on its back and cut a rectangle leaving four strips of the sides of the pan for legs; six holes in the base and the pump was mounted. I hammered the whole thing in between the tapering sides of the bilge beneath the engine.

The hole in the side of the boat for the discharge pipe was more of a challenge: I cut the hole and sealed in the skin fitting. The pipe supplied with the pump was too short!

Of course I should have measured the length required first, and of course it was Sunday so there were no shops open until morning.

Draining the last measure from a whisky bottle I re-deployed the cork to stop up the hole. The cork was too small. So I opened another bottle of whisky… and bought a longer piece of hose in the morning.

But the leak still wasn't cured and I no longer had a frying pan.

There were six other boats in the marina waiting for a good wind to sail southwards, two British and four French. Gathered around the computer in the clubhouse we studied the weather trends, flicking from one web-site to another. Opinions were as varied as the information on the net, but we couldn't deny the wind whistling in the shrouds and flags flying flat and stiff as boards.

Three days later the synoptic charts showed a high pressure area out to the west and the promise of a favourable wind. I motored out towards the open sea, making about two knots into the big swells left over from the storm.

Turning southwards we began to pick up speed. Cape Finisterre's dramatic cliffs slipped by to port, the distant mountains of Galicia disappeared beyond the horizon.

That night the sea was aglow with dense phosphorescence. When dolphins came to play they made fiery trails just below the surface and brilliant splashes that looked just like small explosions. It was easy to imagine how sailors in years gone by might have imagined they'd seen sea serpents.

Phosphorescence!

My dull brain suddenly whirred and clicked into action: the leak!

I lifted the engine cover and saw the little, luminous creatures flowing through the transparent pipes of the cooling system, but not leaking out anywhere. I dismantled the floorboards over the bilge, aft of the engine; I dislodged bags of muesli to inspect the pipe-work and skin fittings around the galley and I poked my head into the space behind the loo. But there was no water or phosphorescent creatures coming in anywhere. Yet still I was pumping ten pumps an hour.

The automatic bilge pump doesn't cut in until the water is about four inches deep, and pumping by hand every hour kept it below that level; I'd forgotten to switch it on anyway.

All through the day and into the next night the sea was uncomfortable. And lonely. No dolphins, no land and not another craft in sight. Sleep came a little easier: I'd set the alarm, doze off within seconds of getting comfortable, and wake up when the bell rang; a quick look around the horizon and back to sleep again. I did this about four times before staying awake long enough to make a log entry and check the engine or sails. At that time of year it was dark for nearly twelve hours, so my pattern seemed to provide sufficient daily rest.

For two more days the wind blew from the north-west, sometimes strong, sometimes gentle, which kept me busy putting in reefs or shaking them out. Cracklin' Rosie will sail just off the wind on the foresail only, so with the sheet slack, lowering the mainsail is quite easy; hoisting it is more difficult: I have to wait for the bow to rise on the back of a wave and ease the pressure on the sail for a moment to get a good pull at the halyard – or start the engine and put her head up.

After two days with the wind blowing from the same direction the waves were getting bigger; I looked again at the ports of refuge along the Portuguese coast, none very attractive with the whole coastline a lee shore.

The new autohelm was working hard to stop the boat from slewing round to windward every time a wave lifted her stern so, following the manufacturer's recommendations, I lowered the main and sailed under poled-out foresail, with the sail to leeward and the pole pushed out between the forward-lower and the cap shrouds. I always use a fore-guy and an after-guy on the pole, as well as a topping lift, that way the foresail can be tacked, gybed or furled without the pole having to be removed first; and there is no danger of it clanging against the shrouds. It's not difficult to rig like that if the lengths of the guys are marked.

When I first learned to sail offshore we always used to sail downwind with the same rig that would be required to sail upwind, so that if someone fell overboard, the boat could instantly turn and beat back upwind without the need to reef or set a smaller foresail. Things have changed: Cracklin' Rosie's genoa can be furled in less than a minute and we have much more reliable engines nowadays.

Besides, if I fell over the side on this trip there was no-one else on board to turn back and pick me up!

Silhouetted against distant clouds backlit by the morning sun, the nearest of the Farilhoes islands climbed over the horizon, then the more distant but higher island of Berlenga; these massive lumps of rock rise out of the sea just south-east of Nazaré Canyon, a deep Atlantic trench which cuts into the Portuguese coastline, where the depth rises from more than three-thousand metres to a hundred or so in less than two miles.

The strait between the islands and Cabo Carvoeiro on the mainland is a little more than five miles wide; we sailed through and I enjoyed writing the entry in the log.

Just around the corner of the cape, on the southern shore, is the little harbour of Peniche, very close and very tempting. But wind from the north was not to be wasted lingering in cafés with wine and food.

I added a few degrees to our course line and sailed on towards Cabo da Roca, the westernmost point of mainland Europe.

Fishing pot markers began to appear in the shallow waters, well marked with sticks and flags, but I wondered about those that might not be so well marked.

Cracklin' Rosie has a long keel, with the propeller neatly tucked away between the after end of the keel and the rudder, so the chances of getting a fishing-pot anchor-line caught around it are so much less than with a modern shaft and 'P' bracket; even so I'd fitted two stainless-steel steps to the transom and one on the rudder just in case I might have to go over the side.

Away to port Cabo da Roca's rough cliffs were beautifully lit by the sun which by now was low in the sky. Five miles further on we rounded Cabo Raso and turned eastwards into the estuary of Rio Tejo, a few miles downstream from Lisbon.

Lights began to show on the shore; I could see the headlights of cars driving along the coast road.

The beam of red light from the lighthouse on the cape changed to white, and its brother, a few miles further along the coast, slowly came into view, guiding us into Marina de Cascais.

285 Miles 2½ Days

Cascais, Portugal
to Santa Cruz de Tenerife, Canary Islands, Spain

I woke with a start: Cracklin' Rosie was surging back and forth, trying to burst her fenders against the edge of the waiting pontoon just inside the Marina entrance. I leapt into the cockpit to check the mooring lines. Out through the entrance I could see huge breakers crashing onto the sandy beach a mile or more away; great clouds of spray thrown up by big waves breaking against the marina wall were flying through the air and spattering across the coachroof. I glanced around quickly to see if I could move the boat somewhere safer.

Then, as suddenly as they'd started, the waves died away. Flags fluttered gently in the breeze, the sun shone and the sea was calm. What created those waves remained a mystery.

Despite my initial discomfort Cascais Marina is a safe place to stay: quiet, beautifully clean and with comfortable facilities; there isn't much social life in the marina though, it's all in the bars and restaurants outside of the security gates, not unlike modern boat-parks at home.

A walk into the old town crosses the plaza (the town square) which is beautifully paved in a black and white mosaic wave pattern - quite stunning and a little disorientating at first sight: the 'waves' create the impression that the pavement undulates all the way across the square. The thought struck me that a visiting sailor making his way back to the marina after an evening in a cafe ashore might think he was walking on water.

The French crews I'd met in Camarinas had arrived in the marina just before me, they were busy cleaning up their boats, getting ready to fly home and go back to work. Two of them came around to say 'au revoir' and pass on what was left in their larders. I ended up with three-hundred 'Cuppasoups'!

I found the leak. Water had been flowing back through the skin fitting, past the flap-valves in the pump and straight into the bilge, but because the pump had still been discharging efficiently that possibility hadn't crossed my mind.

I took out the service kit, removed the pump, dismantled it on the pontoon and fitted new valves and gaskets. Then it didn't work at all. A mild panic later I discovered that the screws holding down the outlet-valve backing-plate, which had come in the service kit, were longer than those I had removed, the valve wasn't seating properly and the pump was sucking air instead of water. Re-assembled with the correct screws it all worked perfectly. I sat on the pontoon in the sunshine delightedly pumping water out of the marina, and back in again. When I refitted the pump I replaced the discharge pipe with a longer one so that, between the pump and the skin-fitting, it looped up higher than the waterline: guaranteed to keep the sea out!

Despite careful cleaning and drying my mobile 'phone was definitely dead. I called home from a public call box; Ida had collected my repaired autohelm from Raymarine in Portsmouth and was planning to deliver it in person to Santa Cruz on the island of Tenerife, my next port of call.

The forecast was for a week of good winds, with a little blip when two cold fronts, one behind the other, were expected to bring seventeen knots of wind from the south for a day; that sounded OK to me and I cast off.

The sun shone and the swells were big, blue, and beautifully gentle. Sailing south, with Cascais far behind on the distant horizon, I chose a job from the (still too long) maintenance list. Like many older boats, Cracklin' Rosie has no fuel gauge. When I'd been forced, by the creeping disintegration of the old one, to have a new fuel tank made, a dipstick was part of the design, but until now it had remained a hidden asset, and useless underneath the fibreglass cockpit moulding where I couldn't get at it. With a cordless drill and a file I cut out a hole through the fibreglass and fitted the little, circular access hatch I'd bought for the job. I folded the hinged, wooden seat back down over my handiwork and, feeling quite self-satisfied, sat back to enjoy the sunset and a glass of wine before dinner. Before the storm.

I don't know whether or not it classified as a proper storm, but the wind went round to the south-west, passed the forecast seventeen knots and kept going, blowing the wrong way for the wave pattern, and me! Without a proper jib, the best course to windward we can make in strong winds, under sail, is about seventy degrees off the wind. I do have a storm jib, but to set it means removing the furled genoa and I really didn't want to sit on the foredeck unfurling and stowing acres of sail. Of course the best way to go to windward in a gale is in a 747, but in a small sailing boat the next best thing is to put three reefs in the mainsail and run the engine. This has a number of advantages and is not as unseamanlike as it might seem: running the engine provides some power in the direction you wish to go, gives the rudder something to bite on when the boat is stopped by a wave and, most importantly, eliminates the chance of seawater running back up the exhaust pipe into the engine which would be disastrous.

Some time later I discussed storm tactics with two charter skippers who regularly sail across the South Atlantic, they said it was their practice too, and for the same reasons.

We tossed and bounced through the night, mostly in an east-south-east direction and on starboard tack, marginally the worst of the two windward options but, theoretically, sailing away from the depression. Twenty-four uncomfortable hours later the first of the fronts had passed and the wind veered. Once more we could sail the course. But we had made no distance towards Tenerife at all.

The sea was still lumpy and uncomfortable but the wind had gone.

I watched a huge, black cloud approach from the west with rain streamers hanging down like ragged, funeral ribbons. Apprehensive, after the bashing we'd been through the night before, I reefed again, climbed back into my foul weather suit and sat there bobbing slowly along, perspiring in my 'oilies' and waiting for the wind to strike.

The cloud passed ahead with no change in the wind at all. If that was the second front it was a minor affair. I ignored a similar cloud that followed and it disdainfully flicked a few droplets of rain at me as it passed.

The sun was hot once the clouds had gone and it was time for lunch: cheese and biscuits with a cup of tea. My small carton of spread was empty so I went forward to get a new tub, which was stowed in a box under one of the bunks in the forepeak. I held the lid of the box open with my elbow, stretched my fingers across the top of the tub and pulled. With a gentle 'click' the tub parted company with the lid and fell to the deck, leaving me with the lid in my hand, melted margarine all over my trousers, in my shoes and flowing slowly into a widening pool beneath the deck boards. There followed a pause for reflection and some calming therapy, which consisted of shouting obscenities at the pool of molten margarine, while I considered how best to deal with the mess. I put down the lid, removed my trousers and piled them, margarine and all, into a handy plastic bag. I reached into the heads compartment for a bundle of toilet paper and rubbed the spread on my shoes into the leather. The deck cleaned up quite easily, and I ate my cheese and biscuits without spread. I towed the trousers behind in an attempt to clean off the worst of the damage, but they were done for.

That night the wind rose again and backed to the SW, the real second front. The pressure didn't change, the wind and sea got worse and sleep was not easy. The rain was as dense as the spray cascading across the deck. I needed the loo (how much more difficult it is for ladies!) and my trousers were leaking. Inside the jacket of my foul-weather gear is a label which states that the suit is waterproof; it wasn't. Sitting on a cockpit cushion a puddle formed around my bottom; water passed through my 'waterproofs' to be soaked up by my sailing trousers and underpants: soggy bottom syndrome.

My carefully plotted great circle route had blown away with the wind and at that point I wanted to go home.

I could picture Ida, sitting in her armchair, feet on the footstool, warm and cosy, reading a magazine or watching TV; and my armchair: dry, comfortable and me not in it.

With three reefs in the main and the engine on again we made a little progress towards Tenerife, still six-hundred miles away. But, as almost always, things looked better in the morning: the wind veered, the sun came out and once more we were making five knots with full main and genny. 'Almost there' I thought.

Suddenly we lurched up to windward, sails flapping and the autohelm whining again. The steering pin on the tiller, a vital connection between the autohelm and the rudder, had broken off. The weld at the bottom of the pin had failed; I watched in disbelief as the broken pin rolled backwards and forwards on the afterdeck.

I steered by hand for a while, wondering how I might solve that little problem.

Then I looked at the hole in the bracket on the tiller, where the pin had been; perhaps not such a problem after all. With a piece of bungee cord as helmsman, Cracklin' Rosie held a fine reach for the three hours it took me to manufacture a new pin: I cut the head off a stainless steel bolt, filed and shaped the shank, drilled out the hole in the bracket and fixed my home-made pin in position with two nuts. We were steering again. Maybe I should carry a spare.

That afternoon I re-learned another lesson: when the wind died completely I started the engine, rolled up the genoa and lowered the mainsail. The boom is quite high when the mainsail is set, so when the sail is lowered the boom hangs on the topping lift and the sheet goes a bit slack.

The boat rolled as I climbed around the sprayhood to get back into the cockpit, the boom swung across and cracked me on the forehead, hard. I lowered myself onto the seat, pulled in the mainsheet, waited for the pain and cursed myself for being so stupid. A bump grew quite quickly and my head ached a little, but there seemed to be no other effects. I do carry a fairly comprehensive medical kit 'but' I said to myself 'that wouldn't be much help if you were unconscious!'

I felt hungry so I concluded that my bodily functions were not impaired and ate some lunch.

Big, smooth swells rolled in from the west but the sea was calm. And it was empty. I had never seen it so empty: no ships, no birds, no dolphins, not even a cloud in the sky. We motored on for hours, then I watched in wonder as night fell and the reflections of brilliant stars illuminated the smooth, undulating surface all around.

Our wake stretched behind, glinting in the starlight, the propeller left a long, glowing trail of phosphorescence beneath the surface.

Cracklin' Rosie's engine is a single cylinder diesel originally designed, I was told, for Chinese fishing boats; it normally needs little maintenance and uses about one litre of fuel an hour. The tank holds twenty litres and I carried fifty litres in cans so, unless we are bashing into strong winds and big waves, we can motor for two hundred and eighty miles.

I checked the fuel level, so easy now with the dipstick, and calculated that with one good day's sailing I could motor the rest of the way to Tenerife if I had to, so we motored on through the night.

The sea was still windless and empty at dawn; it stayed like that until late afternoon when a beautiful, towering bank of white clouds approached from the west. I watched the fluttering wavelets as the wind came. The clouds passed overhead and turned from white to glorious pink and red in the light from the setting sun.

I thought about my hat. I have a white, cotton hat which was quite smart until it gathered a dense layer of mildew. I planned its resurrection. In the early morning light I made up a bowl of bleach solution and dunked the hat; kill or cure.

By afternoon the smart blue band had turned to brown but the mildew had gone. I rinsed out the bleach, less concerned about the use of fresh water now because we'd passed the magical 'one hundred miles to destination' reading on the GPS. The hat dried to nearly as good a shape as it was when new and it has a brim wide enough to shade my neck; the sun burns at this latitude.

I couldn't see it yet but vapour trails from the charter jets as they followed their descent paths to the holiday islands told me that land was not so far away.

That night four ships passed and, in the very early morning, the light from the lighthouse on the north-east corner of Tenerife blinked above the swells.

A little, yellowish, wren-like bird hitched a ride for a while, I hoped we were going his way.

One of the skippers I'd met back in Camarinas had given me the coordinates of 'the best marina in Tenerife'. "You can't miss the entrance" he'd said, "There's a bright green, starboard-hand light and a huge crane." In Santa Cruz there are two marinas fairly close to each other, easily seen from miles away, both have bright green lights and there are huge cranes all along the docks. But the co-ordinates and 'The Canary Islands Cruising Guide' did the trick; I found the entrance to Marina de Santa Cruz, a launch came out to guide me in and helpful hands took our lines.

784 Miles 9 Days

Marina de Santa Cruz

Santa Cruz de Tenerife, Spain
to Mindelo, Sao Vicente, Cabo Verde Islands

Santa Cruz is full of contrasts: old, traditional buildings beside the new; modern artworks and grand, beautiful statues amongst the cactus and palm trees; there are street cafés, supermarkets, news kiosks, ice-cream parlours and, in the backstreets, real shops that specialize in plumbing, ironmongery, and even chandlery! And there is sunshine.

Ida flew in to deliver my new mobile 'phone and the repaired autohelm, and to help with a bit of maintenance: she repaired the sprayhood, reinforced some of the stitching on the cockpit cushions and modified the bimini, which she'd designed and made to provide me with a little shade in the tropics, to stop the corners from flapping in the wind.

My original, very old autohelm - named 'Moaning Minnie' by our sons after the 'moaning' of the electric motor had kept them awake during a long, night haul across the top of Holland - had been behaving erratically, so we contacted the local electronics doctor, Pepe Garcia: he said it was a museum piece he'd like to study and took it away; a couple of days later he brought it back, fixed - after a fashion.

Ida and I lounged in the cafés, enjoyed the sunshine and the delicious coffee, explored the town and crossed off a few more items from the job list.

At the end of our lovely week together Ida caught the bus for the airport and I motored out into the calm of early morning, heading south along the coast.

Tenerife's crowded volcanic peaks were green and brown against the blue of the sky; the fuzzy outline of Gran Canaria, thirty-five miles to the south-east, was just visible through the haze.

By mid-morning the wind filled in and we skipped along, white crests beginning to show on the waves building from behind.

Four dolphins came to play; they were larger than those I had seen off mainland Spain and Portugal, mottled black and grey on their backs but quite white underneath. I ran to the foredeck with my camera but, as usual, the best shots were the ones I missed.

The radio crackled into life: 'Tenerife Traffic' broadcast a weather forecast: 'High pressure over The Azores and a Low over western Africa' which confirmed the forecast of a north-east wind I'd picked up in the internet café the day before. I put 'Moaning Minnie' back to work. Downwind, the old unit draws minimal current because the reaction angle can be increased to about fifteen degrees either side of the desired course, so when the stern is kicked around by a following sea, Cracklin' Rosie's long keel puts her back on track with little reaction required from the helm.

Tenerife's mountains grew smaller and the waves got bigger. I wrapped up the mainsail and furled about a third of the foresail. We were surfing on the crests, and riding up the backs of the waves in front, pointing the bows to the sky then down into the troughs, and going fast -

fast for us that is, about six knots.

I looked back at Tenerife and thought of Ida and our short holiday together; by now she would be in one of those 'planes making white trails across the sky. I could still see Montana Rioja - The Red Mountain - a conical shaped hill on the coast, near the airport; it stands out because its red colour is quite different from its surroundings; I was told that pilots use it as their landfall mark when coming in to land.

There were three unwelcome visitors in the cockpit that night: waves. The first took me by surprise, the sound of a breaking crest racing up from behind was the only warning - it came too late: bubbling water tumbled in over the stern; my shoes were filled, my trousers soaked and the chart table liberally splashed. Years ago I adopted the habit of keeping 'in-use' charts in a transparent, plastic map case, using fine, felt-tipped pens to mark courses and positions, so water on the chart is no more than an inconvenience. I chose not to use electronic charts for this voyage to save money and to help keep battery drain to a minimum; my wind-generator is not efficient when sailing downwind in light winds.

I was ready for the next two visiting waves: washboards in, waterproofs on and my back to the weather. Then a strange or perhaps not so strange phenomenon began to occur: the tiller, pushed by the autohelm, gently nudged my arm, just like a person politely drawing my attention to something and, just for a split second, I reacted. I knew there was no-one else aboard, so there is obviously some psychological explanation for my fleeting feeling. There was another, similar reaction in my mind when my side vision picked up a shadow or a shape that resembled a human form, my 'oilskin' jacket on its hook for example, automatically I looked up to see who it was! This didn't happen more than once in a while, happily, because I felt quite foolish when it did.

All through the night, and the next day, we enjoyed our 'downhill' ride, the wind strength well above the forecast force three or four.

On the evening of the second windy day, as the sun was going down, the whine in the rigging grew louder. I heaved on the furling line to take in some more foresail; the sheet was caught under the anchor chain hawse-pipe (of course); I didn't want to risk yanking on it for fear of pulling out my carefully carved and sanded wooden plug which keeps the sea out of the anchor locker, so I had to go forward. As I bounced and splashed on hands and knees along the side deck I thought: 'if I can be tossed about so casually, why can't the same movements dislodge the sheet?' But that doesn't happen.

Sleep that night was difficult. At one point I took in all sail, the wind was so strong that we were making six knots under bare poles. I wondered why we call it 'bare poles' even when referring to a sloop with only one 'pole'?

Then I did something I'd never done before: I went below for a short sleep. We were rolling and pitching so much that I couldn't wedge myself into a stable position in the cockpit and I really needed some rest. First I took in the spinnaker pole, which I normally leave rigged with topping lift, and guys fore and aft, so that, even when only a scrap of canvas is set, the sail is square to the wind and doesn't back and fill when the boat slews. But now there was a danger that the pole might dip into a wave; the force of the water rushing by could easily break the fore-guy and probably the pole as well, so it had to come in. Sitting on the forehatch, surrounded by tumbling waves, I glanced now and again at the moonlit clouds racing across the sky and marvelled at how we maintained a steady course and remained reasonably upright. I was pleased we did.

Down below, near the centre of the boat, the pitching and rolling has much less effect; I was asleep in seconds, but not for long. I'd forgotten just how loud a wave crashing into the side of the boat can sound below decks; it reminded me of my first trip offshore, in an old, wooden ketch: I'd come off watch and gone below to sleep. The sudden noise was frightening. I thought someone was attacking the bows of the boat with a sledgehammer! I rushed back up to the cockpit to see what we might have collided with, and all was normal; well, as normal as beating into a heavy sea ever is. The skipper reassured me that everything was fine, I went back to my bunk and fell asleep almost instantly.

The alarm went off. I went back topsides, checked what I could see of the horizon, saw no ships and went below again.

Storms pass. In the morning the sun rose amidst billowing, white clouds and the wind dropped to the forecast force four. Slowly the seas subsided and I poled out the foresail again.

I took down the Spanish courtesy flag whilst in the vicinity of the starboard signal halyard and put it back in the flag bag.

My flags are beautiful: hand-made by Ida from discarded, bank cash-bags that I'd collected in the days when such bags were made from coloured cloth. I knew they'd come in handy one day. She'd sat by her ancient sewing machine – bought in the early days of our marriage and still going strong – and diligently copied the colours from my book of flags; she thought the Brazilian flag was very pretty but found it difficult to put together with bits of coloured cloth. I was just grateful to have them.

There were no ships or birds or dolphins that day, or the next. The sea can be an empty, lonely place.

Pressure began to fall again, not quickly but enough to cause a flutter in my sense of well-being, we were still six-hundred miles from Sao Vicente.

Despite the fall in pressure, the dark-grey clouds and me worrying a little, the wind stayed in the north-east and didn't increase all the next day and the next; then the clouds faded away and the sea turned to a beautiful deep-blue, reflecting the clearing sky.

A Tropic Bird, flew alongside for a while, just off to port; I'd never seen one before. They were known to old sailors as 'Bosun Birds' because of their long, thin tail feathers which look a bit like the marlin spikes seamen used when working with ropes.

That night, after the half-moon had set and the stars were bright enough to see by, I lay on my back, staring up at the heavens. Suddenly the boat and the sea around us were brightly illuminated as if by the beam from a lighthouse. I sat up quickly, just in time to see a brilliant, fiery light from the brightest shooting star I have ever seen, falling to earth in the east. Or could it have been a satellite at the end of its life?

Dolphins came again in the morning, about twenty of them,

swimming just under the bows, darting off to one side or the other, leaping or diving so deep that they disappeared except for a flash of white, way beneath the waves.

Four flying fish leapt from the crest of one swell to the next. More life. I wondered if they were fleeing from my dolphins.

Sadly, the next morning there were four little dead ones on the deck. I felt really sorry to think that they might have been escaping from one danger only to run into me, a fatal one.

There had not been a ship or yacht in sight since the Canaries; it was a bit frightening to think of needing help out there in an emergency.

A little niggle began to nibble its way into my consciousness: for a couple of days I'd been hearing a creaking sound from the mast, a noise I hadn't heard before. Twice I'd sat at the foot, trying to locate the source of the sounds but without success. Cracklin' Rosie's mast is strong, made in the days (not so long ago) when such things were a little over-engineered; even so, the sounds were not easy on the ear. The loudest 'creak' I'd yet heard spurred me into action, I determined to identify the cause. I stood on the coachroof and used the foresail halyard, where it exits from the mast, as a handhold while I listened. Ever so slowly my dull brain connected the immediate lack of 'creaks' with the fact that I was pulling on a rope. It was the halyard. Of course there is no need to grind up the foresail as tight as we used to with hanked-on jibs, modern luff-spars keep the sail shape without such strain on muscles and gear, so I relieved a little of the tension and the creaking disappeared.

There was another cause for celebration: we were only fifty miles from Mindelo, we'd be there in the morning.

I decided to take a shower. Although I'd been washing all my important bits with the wet-wipes Ida had given me, I felt a desire to arrive clean and shiny. Cracklin' Rosie isn't big enough to have a built in shower, but I had a Reliance Solar Spray, unused until now because it's an outside unit. The reservoir is a ten litre, black, flexible plastic tank with a protruding pipe which ends in a shower rose. When the unit is hung up in sunshine for an hour or so, the water temperature rises; you stand underneath, open the tap and wallow in the solar heated spray.

I did all the right things: hung the reservoir on the end of the boom, dug out clean clothes, fetched the towel and the shampoo, undressed and turned on the tap. But the rolling of the boat had an unforeseen effect: Sitting naked in the cockpit, looking forward to my shower, I held the rose to direct the spray. I turned on the tap by rotating the pipe where it exits the reservoir. The boat rolled and, because I was holding it, the pipe rotated the other way and the water stopped. I let go of the pipe which then danced about like a ballerina, spraying water all over the place except on me! Then it ran out before I'd washed off all the soap. I had a small whisky instead of a shower.

The wind accelerates between two rocky islands on the northern approach to Mindelo. My pilot book says that some of the navigation lights in the area don't work, so I plotted the course with great care. But the wind was in the right direction and dawn was breaking so we didn't need the lights anyway. I checked my waypoints, checked them again and made fine adjustments to the course as we made our approach.

The waves lifted the stern and drove us forward hard. The rising sun flashed between jagged, volcanic peaks, lighting up the tumbling white horses as we charged into the Canal de Sao Vicente, the channel between the island of Passaro and the main-island shore. I watched the waves crashing into the rocks on either side and swung round into the shelter of the bay on which the city of Mindelo lies.

I turned on the engine, stowed the sails and headed towards the group of yachts anchored in front of the white painted buildings on the shore.

Slowly we meandered into the shallow water, checking the depth, looking for a clear spot close inshore so that I wouldn't have to row too far to reach the land.

A friendly shout from a dinghy heading towards us introduced me to Orlando, one of the 'boat boys' who find work helping visiting yachtsmen. He showed me a good place to anchor, rowed me ashore in his ancient rubber dinghy and, before guiding me through the time-consuming intricacies of 'immigrating', he took me to Club Nautico on the waterfront, where pretty girls serve cold beer, even at ten o'clock in the morning.

850 Miles 9 Days

Mindelo, Sao Vicente, Cabo Verde Islands to Recife, Brazil

Mindelo lies about four hundred and fifty miles to the west of 'the bulge' of Africa. I wandered through the tidy streets, through the park in the middle of town and into tiny shops where my lack of more than a few words of Portuguese had shop assistants puzzled and amused; but everyone was welcoming and friendly.

I read a little about the islands: Darwin didn't like them. I saw only one island and thought it was charming. I learned that The Cabo Verde Islands are now an independent country and part of Africa. Financially they are relatively successful to the point where there is compulsory education and a social welfare structure; and they suffer from illegal immigration, mostly from the African mainland. On shore one morning I was approached by a young man: he asked me to take him to the West Indies; he was personable, educated and an economic migrant searching for a better life. How sad; I couldn't and wouldn't take him to the West Indies but I helped him write a curriculum vitae in English which he could present to the sea freight companies whose ships carry cargo to and from the islands. I wished him luck.

Orlando speaks quite good English and he was a charming companion; he took me on a guided tour of the town and then to the fish market before we walked along the shores of the sheltered bay to a boat builder's yard where a traditional wooden fishing boat, about fifteen metres long, was being built alongside a modern fibreglass launch under repair; of course we ended up in Club Nautico for a beer.

Back on board, after sundown, I'd just washed up the dinner things – not a very onerous task: two small pans and a spoon – when there was a tap on the hull: Orlando's cheerful face appeared in the light from the saloon window. I invited him aboard and we shared a couple of glasses of Drambuie - a drink he'd never heard of - before he rowed back into the darkness towards the boat he was living on, anchored fifty or so metres away.

In the morning I prepared to leave; I waved when Orlando appeared and he rowed over. When I asked him what I owed for his services he just shrugged and said: "whatever you think." I found it difficult to judge but he seemed pleased with what I paid him; it was little enough for such friendly help and companionship

I should have known: the wind was quite gentle in the acceleration zone between the islands of Sao Vicente and Sao Antao, force four and only a few white horses. I shook out some sail, turned off the engine, poured myself a glass of fruit juice and sat back on the cockpit cushions to enjoy the sunshine. Cracklin' Rosie skipped along at about five knots, leaving the rocky, volcanic cliffs well to port.

Mindelo disappeared slowly astern. In the distance, amongst the white buildings along the sea-front, I could see the club, where I'd enjoyed a glass of beer or two, and the fish market where rows of tuna lay on the long, marble slabs waiting to be packed in ice-lined boxes for export.

Leaving behind the shelter of the anchorage, the facilities of the nearby town and Orlando was a little sad, but it was time to go. I was pleased to be on the way again.

Suddenly the wind generator roared, the waves began to toss us about like a pea in a colander and within minutes I was soaked. The steady, north-east trades had veered to the east and accelerated a notch or two. We'd been in the lee of the island and I hadn't noticed the rough water ahead. Some sailor! At least the water is warm at this latitude.

I shortened the mainsail, easier said than done, but the autohelm simply couldn't cope. Every wave that kicked the stern around had the canvas flapping like a flag in a gale, which is pretty well what it was. I hung on to the boom to get the sail down and did little, involuntary dance steps across the coachroof as the waves moved the boat beneath my feet.

My sail plan was dictated by what the autohelm could handle.

The wind and seas gradually eased as we got further south and I stopped thinking about going back and catching the next plane home.

By nightfall, dinner time, we were reaching along at about four and a half knots, still under foresail, and listening to Ella on the CD player.

My Ocean Pilot's advice is to cross the doldrums somewhere near

29° west, so we sailed due south through the night and into the sunshine of the next day, cruising along in the deep, ocean-blue sea.

The course took us close to Ilha Brava, the south-western-most of the Cape Verde group of islands; it was interesting to see how the clouds build up on the windward side of the peaks and evaporate as they roll over the top leaving clear air on the leeward side. Further east, the island of Santiago had a classic halo of cloud about half-way up its slopes.

It would have been fun to stay awhile and explore all the islands in the archipelago, but that would have taken months and I didn't want to miss the southern hemisphere summer.

As night fell a few lights twinkled on the island shore a long way astern.

The wind was slowly dying: I hoisted more sail but within an hour we were becalmed, in the middle of the trade wind belt.

I motored west for a few hours, just in case the lack of wind was due to being in the lee of the island but, conscious of the need to conserve fuel, I gave up, switched off the engine, hoisted the little white light I display when I'm at anchor – not that I could have anchored there, it was three thousand metres deep - curled up and went to sleep.

I woke when the slowly rotating blades of the wind-generator flashed reflections of the morning sunlight into my eyes. A tiny breeze just filled the genoa, we were moving again.

Clouds on the eastern horizon hinted at more wind from that direction, and it came. All through that day and the next night we reached along with one reef in the mainsail and a matched foresail.

At dawn the next morning the rising sun lit a big, black cloud and turned it to an angry orange colour which was reflected on the surface of the waves; we were on a collision course. I pulled in the third reef and rolled up a little more foresail; the big, black cloud sauntered over the masthead and nothing happened. Oh well, I'd rather reef and not need it than have too much sail up in a blow.

I was looking forward to enjoying my breakfast until I tasted the long-life milk, it was sour: I usually take a tiny, taster-sip from the carton, to make sure that it's still good, before pouring it over my muesli. I sipped: ugh! It was horrible. I spat it out over the side. Then I looked at the words on the carton: it was grapefruit juice.

I had a change of menu for dinner that day: minced beef and onions instead of my favourite which is rice with fried onions and baked beans, with a little curry powder for added flavour. Heinz beans are, outstandingly in my opinion, the best tasting baked-beans-in-tomato-sauce you can buy; nutritionists have told me that they are almost a complete diet.

Most of the tinned food from supermarkets is pretty tasty these days too, and meal-sized tins with ring-pull tops make very little waste or mess. Chicken in white sauce is very good; beef and chicken stews provide a taste of potato now and again. Rice is by far the easiest bulk-food to go with the main ingredient; it uses only the exact amount of water required, so is economical with the liquid that is so precious when there's no mains supply.

I eat muesli for breakfast, with milk and chopped fresh fruit if it's available; powdered milk, at a rate of two heaped desert spoons per helping of cereal, with added water, is tasty enough too; so is tinned fruit which, if you drain the juice and drink that separately, also goes well with cereal.

At lunchtime I have some kind of biscuit, often with cheese and olives, sometimes with tinned meat and sometimes with honey or jam. I drink frequent mugs of tea and coffee, water, fruit juice, and drinking chocolate at night. It's a pity that drinking chocolate manufacturers don't sell their product in containers more suited to the rough and tumble of the food cupboard of a small yacht at sea. Biscuits, cookies and cakes, usually provided by kind ladies who think I need looking after, are good for snacks, so is chocolate – although it melts at about the same latitude as milk turns sour and margarine turns to liquid.

I hadn't seen a dolphin for days; I wondered if the apparent lack of marine life was my fault for not looking around often enough; there could have been columns of whales filing past whilst I was peeling onions. I decided to have a dedicated observation hour every day before dinner. On the first evening of the new regime I stood in the cockpit, poised, camera ready, and saw two flying fish, too far away and flying too fast for photos; there was an apparent increase in the number of Storm Petrels, but nothing else.

The wind was dying again. 'Must be in the doldrums' I thought. Surrounded by huge, grey clouds with rain streamers hanging down beneath them, we pottered along under engine whilst I struggled with the dilemma of which course to steer.

The pilot book explains that in the Atlantic Ocean, just south of the equator, the further east you are the more southerly the wind direction; further west the wind comes from the south-east.

So the question I struggled with was whether to sail due south, to meet the predicted southerlies sooner, or suffer the fluky conditions for longer, get further west and meet the wind from a more favourable direction.

I argued with myself.

"What's the wind doing now?"

"Nothing."

"What's it doing further west?"

"Probably the same."

"Where's the nearest wind likely to be?"

"Due south from here."

"Sure?"

"That's what the pilot book says."

"Best head south then, we can always bear away a bit towards the west if it's strong from the south."

"That's what I said in the first place!"

I chose the southerly course. We motored through the day, I topped up the tank, and we motored through the night.

At dawn the sky ahead was filled with fluffy, white, trade-wind-type, cumulus clouds and I began to hope that we were approaching the steady winds predicted on the charts. A breeze ruffled the surface; it grew stronger, strong enough to sail; but it came from the north east again; did that mean we hadn't crossed the doldrums at all? And so much fuel used motoring through the calms, Recife still a thousand miles away.

I set a course just west of south and sailed straight into a traffic jam:

a ship crossed ahead from starboard to port, and about forty dolphins rushed towards the boat, leaping and spinning; some of them even attempting horizontal spins, crashing sideways into the waves when they couldn't complete the spin. Magnificent! They must have been enjoying themselves; they certainly gave me great pleasure.

When the ship and the dolphins had gone I made some lunch and wondered again about the best course. The wind was definitely not following the instructions in my books.

The east wind died and we wallowed in rolling, silver-grey sea.

I'd been looking forward to the doldrums as an area of enforced inactivity, time to read or paint; but in the event I found it frustrating: rolling from side to side in the swells and going nowhere; sails and halyards flapping loosely, making an irritating clatter as they banged against the mast.

Huge clouds were building in the east again, some of them very beautiful, others with the darkest of dark rain streamers hanging down to the sea. The darkest one, with the blackest rain, hovered overhead for a while, just long enough to ensure that my recently dried trousers and shirt were thoroughly wet again.

The hot sun between the clouds dried me as we drifted along. All day, through the night and into the morning I set and re-set the sails to meet little changes in wind direction. Slowly we made headway.

A flash of iridescent blue made me look up; my brain's instant recognition retrieval system came up with 'kingfisher' but of course it was a flying fish, and what a beauty: it had a brilliant turquoise body with ruddy, almost red wings; it skipped from wave crest to wave crest, sometimes a metre or more from the surface. 'How odd' I thought, 'that nature produces birds that swim and dive and fish that fly'.

The evening brought an almost tranquil peace – at first: I was dozing in the cockpit, safety harness clipped on by the way, when a dollop of rain, as big as a ping-pong ball, landed 'splosh' on my forehead. An instant later there was a brilliant flash of lightning and an ear-shattering clap of thunder, the boat heeled to 45° and the sails thrashed about as if trying to shake the mast down. Rain poured down in a deluge and there was wild blackness all around.

Quickly I furled the foresail, leaving just enough to give the autohelm a chance, grabbed two sail ties and crawled forward to the mast.

I noticed one little thing in my favour: the howling wind – what strength it was I can only guess at – had veered before it struck, which meant that I didn't have to change course for the sail to be flapping about freely enough to be pulled down. But it wasn't easy: the wild water made Cracklin Rosie's motion so violent that I dared not chance using both hands: I clung to the wet, slippery mast with my right and dragged the sail down, bit by bit, with my left, grateful that I knew where everything was without the need for light. Finally I managed to wrap a sail tie around the billowing canvas. The worst was over.

Back in the cockpit I sheeted in the boom and tidied the dangling reefing lines: relative peace. Relative because the wind had quickly built up a sharp chop and we were still being thrown around like a bucking bronco rider. We crashed forward into the waves, flinging buckets of spray along the deck, driven by the scrap of foresail I'd left flying.

Earlier I'd been thinking about rigging the shower again. I hadn't taken the shower gel from my wash bag, but by now I was thoroughly soaked and I think I was thoroughly clean; it was like being in a power shower only fully dressed.

More rain fell, torrents. I hid below, sliding open the hatch every so often to check around the horizon, not that I could see much; but we'd seen only one fishing boat and a tanker since leaving the Cabo Verde islands so I didn't feel that we were in much danger.

So it went on, through the most uncomfortable night I've ever spent at sea, suffering with the crashing and banging of everything that wasn't firmly tied down or jammed somewhere; pitching and rolling wildly. I wondered anxiously how the mast and rigging could stand such abuse.

By morning the sea had calmed a little: the motion was easier and, wonderfully, the wind had settled in the southeast. Not only that, we were almost on the equator.

At 1039 UT on 27 November 2005 I started to pour a small libation to the King of The Sea; then I thought: 'I don't really believe there's a king down there' so I drank the rest myself.

I tried to capture the moment on the GPS with a photo but only managed 00° 00'.002S; then I realised that I could have set the reading to zero in harbour and taken the photo in comfort! But that would have been cheating. Never mind, we'd made it into the southern hemisphere and, for the first time in my life, I put an 'S' after the latitude in the log.

The distance to Recife was now less than 600M but it wasn't going to be plain sailing: for the next three days dense rain fell from great lumps of cloud galloping by overhead, the wind backed and veered, strengthened, weakened and kept me fully occupied putting in reefs and shaking them out again; gradually it steadied and blew from about east-south-east, which was perfect. We were on the home run.

Two more days and Brazil appeared as a glow in the sky above the night horizon, patrolled by numerous fishing boats showing only their fluorescent, white lights, following, in the way of fishing boats, no regular course.

We were nearly there. As the sun rose the glow in the sky became a long, grey smudge of land which gradually turned into low hills with clusters of high-rise buildings at intervals along the shore.

I hoisted the 'Q' flag and the Brazilian courtesy flag, excited about being close to land and on my first visit to a country in the southern hemisphere.

The harbour walls which protect the city of Recife from the sea began to take shape, as things always do when you get closer.

I'd forgotten that in the Americas green channel marker buoys are red, and reds are green; the overlapping walls of the northern entrance to the harbour had me confused for a moment or two, not least because my attention was taken by a sharp line we were about to cross where the colour of the sea changed from ocean blue to seaweed green; I thought later that it must have been the line where the fresh water from the Recife's rivers meets the salty, ocean seawater.

A small sailing boat beating out of the harbour entrance identified the way for me. I motored alongside to ask directions; it was a sailing school boat and the distraction caused the student helmsman to make an involuntary tack, but the instructor was friendly and helpful and shouted directions, in English! A mile or so down the harbour a group of yachts on buoys or at anchor were the signpost for the Pernambuco Iate Clube (yacht club).

A man in a small boat rowed out to meet me and attached my mooring line to a buoy.

Before long I was sitting on the clubhouse veranda with a cold beer.

1744 Miles 18 Days

Recife to Rio de Janeiro

Recife means 'reef' in Portuguese; the city is named after the long ridge of rock, nearly two miles in length, which protects the harbour from the rolling Atlantic waves. A wall has been built along the top of the ridge to make it a little higher; breaking seas crash against the rocks sending cascades of spray over fishermen leaning on the wall, but in the harbour all is peace and calm even in the strongest winds.

The yacht club, about halfway along the reef, dates back to 1884 when it was a restaurant with a salt water swimming pool; in 1902 the restaurant was burned down by, it is said, wives of the gentlemen who dined there who considered the female staff to be unsuitable companions for their husbands!

A club for small boat sailors was formed on the site in 1949; now it runs the longest sailing race in Brazil, from Recife to a volcanic island called Ilha Fernando de Noronha and back, a round trip of six hundred miles.

The club welcomes visitors too.

Negu, who'd helped me tie up when I arrived, took me into the city to deal with the formalities: we walked half a mile further along the reef to an area dotted with unusual art works and an ornamental column commemorating the turn of the millennium.

I stopped for a while and took some photo's; I couldn't make my mind up whether or not I liked the (to me) strange objects, geese with human feet for example, but they were certainly arresting.

From a short jetty at the water's edge we boarded a small, wooden dinghy; a cheerful ferryman rowed us across the harbour, the fare was pennies.

On the far side we climbed worn, stone steps, up to a wide, open plaza and lines of traffic roaring along a main road.

Recife is a big, bustling city at the conjunction of three rivers; over two million people live there, I think I met most of them: street vendors, musicians, purveyors of coconuts, lottery ticket sellers, pretty peanut-vendors and just people, everywhere.

Negu and I had lunch in a street cafe where the jolly proprietress pulled tables and chairs from stacks by the wall and extended her seating capacity along the pavement and out into the road!

We were approached, as we ate, by people selling watches, lighters, jewellery, sunglasses, and some who wanted to clean my shoes; it could have been a nuisance but they were all good humoured when we said 'no thanks'.

Visiting the police station, the harbourmaster, the health department and the immigration office was next on the menu: I took my passport, health certificate, boat registration documents, insurance papers, passport photos and my crew list with just one name on it. It wasn't easy: the officials were all helpful but the offices were all in different parts of the city and they opened at different times; even with Negu's help it took three days to 'immigrate' - on my own it would have taken much longer.

Each evening, after plodding through the streets in the energy-sapping heat I was glad to take the little ferry back across the harbour for a quiet beer in the yacht club.

I stayed in Recife for a week; I explored a little of the city, listened to the music and bought some peanuts. It was time to go. Surprisingly the only clearance necessary for departure was to call the harbour radio station on the VHF radio to let them know; I doubted that the information would reach all the departments where my arrival details had so laboriously been registered. I left quietly in the early morning.

Heading south outside the harbour wall I switched on the autohelm; it whined. I pressed all the buttons and still it whined; the idea of naming it 'Whining Winnie' crossed my mind but it wasn't a friendly machine so it remained an 'it'.

I rigged the repaired unit that Ida had delivered to Tenerife and set the course.

Slowly the Brazilian coast changed from great clusters of skyscrapers beneath towering clouds to low, wooded hills stretching into the hazy distance.

All day the steady wind drove us southwards, just as the pilot book predicted.

A shoal of silver flying fish leapt from under the bow and scuttled away to hide in the next wave.

Fishing boats turned on their bright, fluorescent lights as the golden sun went down behind the hills.

The alarm rang every twenty minutes and I dozed through the night.

We were heading straight across the wide bay on which Salvador lies, about five-hundred miles from headland to headland; by mid-morning we were alone on the ocean again.

I checked the sails and the steering and made some coffee. The wind swung round to the east; our course was just west of south so we were rolling. I carefully noted the technique required to keep the coffee from surging into my nostrils: sitting on the starboard side of the cockpit, I waited for the boat to roll that way then put the cup to my lips as the roll back to port commenced and finished the sip before passing the vertical.

Sometimes the rolls were too sharp or were interrupted by a rogue wave, either of which could result in spills, stains, and coffee up my nose.

That afternoon fifty or more dolphins appeared from nowhere and charged towards the boat from all directions; it was quite dramatic. I rushed to get the camera; they stayed for more than an hour, jumping, diving and darting back and forth under the bow. I wondered if it was the young males that made the most spectacular leaps, showing off.

By now the sun was almost directly overhead at mid-day and I was glad of the little bimini that Ida had made. I used plenty of sun cream and covered up fairly well, but the burning rays sneaked in here and there. I took to wearing a small towel, dangling from beneath my hat, to cover my neck; I should have thought of that earlier.

Days passed with little change in wind direction or strength; we reached along through blue sea, beneath the sun or the stars and saw, on average, one ship per day and very few birds.

About six-hundred miles south of Recife the Abrolhos Archipelago much of which is just below the surface, extends to about forty miles offshore; I set the course to pass well clear to seaward of the rocks not least of all because of the possibility of currents and disturbed seas.

We passed the easternmost point of the shallows at about 0200, six days out from Recife. Other vessels were turning there too; the sea was suddenly busy with up to six ships in sight at any one moment. I turned slightly off the straight-line route, back towards the coast and quieter waters as soon as I could.

After days of sunshine, with the occasional shade of a passing cumulus, a dark, grey morning came, full of clouds and falling rain. I knew that Brazil has extensive rain forests so I supposed rain could be expected from time to time.

But this morning it was inconvenient: I'd finished my tea and muesli, run up the engine to charge the No 2 battery after the night's drain, and was about to wash and clean my teeth when the cloud I'd been watching over the starboard quarter made a sudden advance. Within seconds rain was dancing on the waves all around us.

A ship appeared from behind a shower further downwind, some distance off but heading in our direction; visibility was decreasing rapidly, and we were on a probable collision course.

The ship disappeared from view.

I discussed the options with the crew:

"Should I stand on and rely on having been seen and the collision avoidance regulations being applied?"

"Should I turn to starboard?"

And if we'd been seen: "Would the ship's captain decide to turn to port as the quickest route away from the closest point of approach?"

The general consensus of opinion was 'turn to starboard'.

I started the engine, sheeted in the mainsail and turned 70° which put me at a near right angle to the last-seen track of the ship.

We were enveloped in dense, dark blankets of rain, so heavy that the falling drops made the spinnaker pole 'ping' like a bell! I tried ineffectively to shelter under the spray hood, but with the possibility of thousands of tons of nasty, hard steel suddenly bursting into view I didn't dare hide below.

Minutes passed.

The dark cloud swept by overhead, leaving a curtain of drizzle.

The ship reappeared about half a mile astern; it hadn't changed course at all.

The rain cleared and, after seven days and nights out of sight, Brazil appeared once more, grey and undulating, in the west. We were in less than thirty metres of water; the sea had turned green again.

Oil and gas platforms squatting just above the waves were scattered across the horizon ahead; chatter on VHF radio indicated an increase in the number of vessels nearby and my sleep pattern was reduced to frequent, short catnaps. Rio de Janeiro was still two days sailing away until a sudden, unexpected increase in wind strength meant a welcome increase in speed.

Rio looked a lot closer at six knots than it did at four, but it didn't last. The wind died at dusk; a mass of dense clouds gathered and a spectacular display of lightning filled the sky; there was almost no sound, only brilliant, continuous light, sometimes white and so bright that it almost hurt, sometimes a grey, tinged with orange that highlighted the fantastic shapes of the clouds all around us.

The drama continued. I gave up watching for a while to cook myself some dinner. I ate with a cabaret performing but, sadly, no wine. All through the night the electrical display continued until hazy, morning light painted cliffs and sky as a background to the flashes as the storm slowly moved away to the north.

Cabo Frio, the last headland before Rio jutted out from the land ahead. Close inshore a dark shape was silhouetted against the cliffs; it was moving. I stared, wondering what it could possibly be, until I gave in and went below for the binoculars, then I could see it as the conning tower of a submarine; the hull was invisible just below the horizon. I half expected a visit from the Brazilian Navy, but they ignored me.

Beyond the cape a breeze set in from the north-east and for the first time since leaving The Solent we had wind and flat water, luxury! But it soon fell away to nothing.

The sea took on a misty, grey hue and we slowly rose and fell on swells from distant winds. Not a ripple showed on the surface. We motored through the hot day and on into the night.

The white and red lights marking the entrance to Rio harbour were visible for a long, long time; I watched, envious of their speed, as two ships overtook us and turned in towards the city.

Then it was our turn; we motored in past the dark silhouette of the famous Sugar Loaf Mountain, where James did battle with 'Jaws' on top of a cable car in one of the Bond movies, and headed for a gap between the headland and an island a little way offshore. The echo-sounder showed three hundred metres, 'that's a bit too deep' I thought; then it changed to thirty metres - which was closer to the depth shown on the chart - then three metres, then sixty, then back to three hundred again; clearly it had a headache.

I slowed and aimed at the middle of the gap remembering, as I did so, the words of Colonel Stan Townsend who was the Chief Instructor at the British Kiel Yacht Club where I gained my first skipper's ticket back in 1974. At that time none of the training boats there had echo-sounders which had worried me a little when I turned up for my week's course and exam.

"Wouldn't it be better if we had echo-sounders sir?" I'd asked. He looked at me sternly; then he said: "If you navigate properly you'll know where you are; if you know where you are you'll know how deep the water is; why do you need an echo-sounder?"

Well, I knew where I was and I knew how deep the water should have been. I crept though the gap, swung around the headland and found a peaceful anchorage in a quiet corner of the harbour.

1073 Miles 10 Days

Rio de Janeiro to Rio Grande

When I woke I hauled in the anchor and motored the short distance down to the Rio Yacht Club - famous in sailing history – and tied up in their little harbour. The man in the office very politely told me that they didn't accommodate visitors; I was surprised - no, shocked - and disappointed. I pointed out that there were a number of unoccupied mooring buoys but he was adamant. At least they gave me a cup of coffee.

I cast off and headed for Marina da Gloria which had been identified for me on the chart in the office. Sailing boat masts poked up behind the curving breakwater. I motored in and tied up on a vacant pontoon; but before diving into the shower I spent a while fiddling with the echo-sounder: I switched it on and off and on again, turned the gain control up and down, flicked between shallow range and deep range; and still it jumped from one depth to another and back again. Back to basics. An unreliable echo-sounder is worse than no echo sounder at all; I threw it away.

The marina is comfortable and safe, with immaculate facilities; expensive too: about forty-five pounds per night for my little Twister! It lies conveniently close to the city but separated from it by a wide, sweeping park which borders the curve of the bay. Trees in the park were full of flowers, their fallen blooms splashed the lawns with many colours.

There was no coverage for my mobile 'phone anywhere in Brazil but one of the little shops in the marina complex sold me a card; I spent twenty minutes working out how to make an international call from a public 'phone booth, and called home. It was lovely to talk with Ida and hear how our grandchildren were progressing; I have pictures of them all in a frame on the forward, saloon bulkhead. Of course I had to discuss the echo sounder problem as well; by the time I rang back a couple of days later a new one was on order.

My bird recognition was improving: I saw green sparrows as I strolled through the park towards the centre of Rio de Janeiro, yellow ones too but they flew away when I was approached by two uniformed policemen who warned me not to carry my camera in the 'holster' on my belt: "Too visible" they said "and too attractive to thieves."

A map from the tourist information office guided me to the police station where I tried to book in with the authorities; I was politely redirected to a branch office about half a mile away, where I was sent back to the first one, from where I was sent back again. I gave up and became an illegal immigrant.

If Recife bustles, Rio hustles! Loaded with bags full of groceries from a supermarket, I took a taxi back to the marina. We joined the eight-lane dual-carriageway at about eighty miles an hour then caught up with the rest of the traffic! The scenery was a blur, buses changed lanes to overtake without warning; horns blared, brakes squealed and my bones rattled.

The city is impressive: overlooked by the famous statue of 'Christ The Redeemer' and the Sugar-Loaf Mountain, it is busy, colourful and noisy; there are palm lined avenues, restaurants, cafés, and many fine buildings, one of which is the Naval Club which I entered quite by chance: I stood admiring the rather grand entrance and was invited in by Eduardo, one of the club guides who happened to be standing on the steps near the doors at the time; he told me that the building was open to the public, he was a new employee and, if I agreed, he would practise his tour presentation on me. He showed me around the beautiful rooms and halls, rich with paintings illustrating the history of the harbour and the Brazilian navy, and statues to rival the best of galleries. We finished the tour in a nearby café with a beer and some lunch. From there, at Eduardo's suggestion, I walked across the road to the city's fine-art museum which is a spacious, silent gallery where I spent an hour admiring some really good paintings by artists I'd never heard of.

That was enough culture for one day so I wandered back to the marina.

Sounds of chatter and laughter floated across the water as I stepped onto the walkway between the mooring pontoons: my neighbours on the boat 'next door' were having a party; they invited me aboard and forced me to drink a few glasses of their extremely good, home-made fruit punch. Eight of us were squeezed into the cockpit so it was quite friendly. They all spoke pretty good English - which improved noticeably as the level in the punch-bowl went down, as did my Portuguese.

I left with fond farewells and stepped across the pontoon to get some sleep; I was leaving in the morning.

All was quiet next door when I woke; I left a 'thank-you' note on the deck by the companionway and cast off, sorry to leave, as usual, but glad to be moving again - until I got to the fuel jetty, where the swell rolling in through the harbour entrance met the force of a nearby stream flowing out from under the jetty. Tied up alongside I thought the cleats were going to be torn from the deck as we heaved away from the wooden structure and then crashed back against the row of tyre fenders; but I had to have fuel. I clung on with one hand and held the filler nozzle with the other, squirming at the creaking and straining of my mooring lines.

After that I really was glad to get away.

Out towards the lovely, offshore islands I waved as we sailed past Ipanema, in case she was watching. From the words of the song I'd always had a mental picture of a beautiful, sun-tanned girl strolling past weather-beaten, timber cabins set amongst grassy sand-dunes; the reality was a bit different: Ipanema does have a long, sandy beach but with densely packed, high-rise blocks of concrete instead of sand dunes. I waved anyway. Maybe she waved back.

Contrary to the forecast, the wind came from the north not the south. We were soon broad reaching through the afternoon, with the foresail poled out to leeward in order to stop it filling and collapsing.

Watching the sun go down I wondered why, if we were steering 245° which we were, was the sun setting dead ahead? Surely on 23 December at 23° south it should be setting pretty well due west? I thought about it for a moment then got on with other things, reasonably confident that the sun was still in the right place in the sky. Later, I checked the amplitude tables and discovered that neither the sun nor the compass were in error. I drew a diagram on a scrap piece of paper and illustrated to myself why the compass certainly should have been reading 245° - how silly of me to have thought otherwise.

The wind went away in the morning, and we motored all through the hot, sultry day.

Late in the afternoon the wave pattern did set in from the south and a light breeze from a little further east. I hoisted the mainsail and we made an uncomfortable three knots motor sailing into the night.

We had burned a lot of fuel so soon after setting out that I was faced with a decision: whether to stay close to the shore and find some fuel in a fishing harbour, or steer a straight line course to our planned destination.

In the end the wind chose for me.

My friendly neighbour in the marina had commented on how lucky they are in Brazil: sunshine most of the time and never any really strong winds. Now the rigging was singing; I reefed and reefed again. By the time I'd put in the third reef it was dark and the wind was howling; at least it wasn't cold. We were heading to seaward of my desired course, making four knots on a close reach.

I'd worked out that in the southern hemisphere sailing on a port tack ought to lead away from a depression. We were on starboard. But as the barometer rose with the sun, the wind backed, I tacked, and we were on course again.

A note I'd made in the log reminded me that it was Christmas Day; I almost hadn't noticed. Then I thought of Ida and our children, and grandchildren who would be sitting on the floor in our sitting room, laughing and shouting amid piles of discarded wrapping paper.

That day I made the stove work properly - my Christmas present to myself.

The Taylor's paraffin stove was one of the features which influenced my choice when I bought Cracklin' Rosie: the advantages of world-wide availability of fuel, no danger of explosion and relative ease of maintenance were very attractive. But despite a 'factory overhaul' the pressure tank had refused to maintain pressure for long enough to boil a pan of rice. It hadn't stopped working so wasn't high priority on the job list; I'd been looking at it threateningly on and off for the past few weeks. Having made all the obvious checks, I'd finally identified a leaking valve in the pressure tank as the culprit. When I called home from Recife I'd explained to Ida exactly which valve I needed and faxed a diagram from the marina office.

When I called from Rio the answer was disappointing: they don't make that kind of valve any more.

The valve that was leaking sits at the bottom of the pressure pump tube; it's a hand operated pump, the handle of which protrudes from the side of the cylindrical tank – the valve wouldn't get many stars for ease of access. I took a long screwdriver, loosened the valve retaining screw, then bent a stiff piece of wire and hooked it under the head of the valve body, unscrewed a couple more turns and lifted the valve out. A tiny, carefully cut, rubber valve seat made the repair and, after reassembly, I could boil a kettle again without having to pump up the pressure half-way through the process.

The course I'd planned took us fairly close to Cabo de Santa Maria Grande. Just inshore of the cape, to the north, is a little harbour called 'Laguna', where the waters of the San Antonio lagoon meet the sea.

Hoping to find some fuel I headed for the entrance.

The wind was onshore. We approached on a dead run. It soon became clear that the lagoon was emptying or the tide was ebbing, or both: the waves grew bigger and steeper and with no detailed chart I began to worry a little about the possibility of shallows where the ebbing waters meet the sea. Through the binoculars I spied some large fishing boats moored well inside the harbour and concluded from that observation that the water ought to be deep enough for my little boat; I let the autohelm steer us while I stood at the shrouds swinging the lead-line to make sure that it was.

We rolled and bounced our way in; I was amused by pairs of dolphins playing around the end of the northern mole, wondering how, in such big waves, they avoided the huge, granite blocks.

Once inside the shelter of the harbour the water was calm. Rows of fishermen standing in the shallows with nets ready to cast watched silently as we motored past. I've since learned that this is part of the only known instance of animals deliberately working with humans. The fishermen work as a team with a local pod of bottlenose dolphins: the men wait in the shallows while the dolphins round up the fish and drive them towards the beach. The dolphins then roll on their sides, which the fishermen take as the cue to cast their nets. Any fish that escape the nets swim straight into the mouths of the waiting dolphins!

I motored in as far as the row of fishing boats moored against a quay on the northern bank, but there was no sign of a fuel berth and no-one around to ask.

Back nearer to the entrance 'Geraldo's Restaurant', on the southern bank, had white painted tyres tied along its balcony which I took as an indication that boats might tie up there. I came alongside, rigged mooring lines, climbed onto the balcony, said 'good afternoon' and asked for a beer.

It turned out that the only diesel available was at a garage in the town on the other side of the river, where there was nowhere to tie-up; it would have been too time consuming to blow up the dinghy for a ferrying operation so I settled for the beer. Geraldo came to join me at the table; I could easily have stayed for more than one. He helped with my lines when I cast off and insisted on presenting me with a couple of cans of lager 'for the journey'.

We motored out through the steep swells, the point of the foredeck scooping up great dollops of sea and hurling them aft to splash over the cockpit coaming and into my shoes.

Out beyond the cape the shoreline stretched into the distance and gradually fell away below the horizon. The western sky was a deep, deep red and the wind had gone further into the north, a good direction but it was cold! Surely a north wind at this latitude should be warm?

I made some supper and sat in the cockpit listening to music before putting in the washboards and closing the hatch, just in case any of the waves surging up behind us decided to come aboard.

My night attire was foul-weather gear.

The safety precautions turned out to be unnecessary; dawn came with about force three, still from the north but much warmer now.

Not long into the day the sun began to burn; once more I was pleased to have my little bimini.

Gradually the low, grey coastline re-appeared through the surface haze. Slowly we closed the shore, and slowly the wind died.

We motored through four distinct lines of a reddish-brown substance on the surface of the sea which formed stringy strands when disturbed. I was mildly concerned that it might affect the engine cooling system but water continued to emit from the exhaust and the engine didn't falter.

I've seen similar, slightly redder streaks in the English Channel; it's algae.

The hot day passed and we motored on into the night, the engine thumping away, driving us along at about four knots.

In the early morning light the eastern arm of Rio Grande harbour gave me a visible aiming mark. The watchkeeper in the pilot station answered my radio call and gave me directions to the yacht club.

A wide, deep river connects the sea to 'Lagoa dos Patos' the enormous lagoon on which Rio Grande lies; it is the biggest lagoon in Brazil, over twenty-five miles long. 'Patos' is believed to be the name of an indigenous tribe that were living in the area when Europeans arrived.

Warehouses and cranes are dotted along the southern bank, most had merchant ships moored beneath the overhanging jibs.

The opposite side of the river is shallow, with banks of reeds and little, tree covered islands.

Long lines of twenty or thirty cormorants flew across our bows as we motored inland, dolphins broke the surface and birds dived for fish all around us for almost all of the ten miles upstream to the town. Fishermen in their small, traditional craft and men working on the light on a buoy pointed out the route between the islands when I slowed alongside and asked.

The Rio Grande Yacht Club is just beyond the town, in a small creek amongst fields and reed beds, peaceful and beautiful.

I came alongside the end of a jetty, someone took my bowline and, with Cracklin' Rosie safely tied up, I walked up to the club restaurant where I met Tomaz and Ester – 'chief cook and bottle washer' - who immediately gave me a meal. The club administrator came over to say 'hello' and invited me to stay as long as I wanted saying that there would be no charge. What delightful welcome and what a contrast to the yacht club in Rio de Janeiro.

803 Miles 8 Days

Rio Grande, Brazil to Puerto Madryn, Argentina

It was New Year's Day. Rio Grande was quiet when I wandered into town; rows of silent fishing boats were moored side by side along the town quay, a few old men sitting on a low wall by the water nodded a greeting as I passed.

The lagoon stretches inland between banks of reeds; not a wave rippled the surface except where diving birds splashed into the silvery-grey water.

I walked along dusty pavements beside buildings set out in rectangular blocks with wide streets between them. Weeds with pretty flowers grew from gaps between the paving stones. A Brazilian flag hung from a pole in front of a wooden hut behind a long, stone wall. Built into the wall, near the gate, was a bas-relief of Lord Baden-Powell and the name of the scout group which I assumed used the hut as their headquarters; I marvelled at the distance his influence had travelled.

I stayed for three days at the friendly yacht club; each evening Tomaz and Ester produced some tit-bit from the kitchen for me; our conversations were limited: my Portuguese vocabulary and their few words of English were soon exhausted, but with drawings on paper napkins and lots of hand signals they asked me where I'd come from, where I was going and told me how to 'phone home.

On my last day there I found a taxi, filled my empty diesel cans and ferried them back to the boat. I shook hands with Tomaz and Ester and left a 'thank you' letter in the club office.

There were long, red streaks across the sky behind the moored yachts when I left in the morning; some of the fishing boats from the town had cast off too, others passed us on their way to the sea as we motored down-river, a good sign I thought.

A sea lion surfaced and snorted at me as we left the shelter of the harbour; the sun broke through the thin layer of haze and a gentle wind blew from the south, gradually backing and increasing in strength until, by evening, we were almost sailing the course with two reefs in the main and a half-rolled foresail; but it didn't last.

Just as the sun was setting a big, dark cloud approached; as it passed the wind backed 50° instantly! I was about to shake out a reef and let out more foresail when, just as quickly, it veered back to its previous direction and a bit more; we made dismal progress to windward. I put the engine on.

By morning nothing had changed.

Just after lunch I did a serious progress check: since leaving Rio Grande harbour we'd covered one hundred and twenty miles over the ground and made seventy-five miles in the direction we wanted to go.

I had a serious look at the options: I could go back but didn't want to; I could anchor in shallower water but, closer to the shore, the waves were short, steep and uncomfortable so I didn't want to do that either.

But we couldn't motor all the way to Cape Horn so we sailed, tacking through about 120 degrees in the empty, rolling sea.

On one tack I took us inshore, to have a closer look at the coast. Eighty miles south of Rio Grande the beautiful, sandy beach stretches for miles and miles, backed by forest and splashed by the (usually) blue Atlantic, it is totally empty. I wondered how long it would be before tourist hotels line the shore.

As the day wore on, the wind and waves grew quieter. Fishing boats turned on their lights; so did I and we sailed on through the night.

The morning sun struggled weakly through grey clouds onto a grey sea. I was dozing in the cockpit when the sound of an engine shook me awake: a big fishing boat was heading directly towards us. Before leaving England I'd thought about the possibility of being boarded by pirates or even being kidnapped and held for a ransom.

I'd listened to advice ranging from taking a gun to just being totally passive. No one I spoke to had ever experienced any contact with pirates, so in the end I decided that if it should happen I'd react to the circumstances as they occurred. I didn't have a gun.

These thoughts flashed through my mind as the fishing boat drew near but it didn't look unfriendly; the skipper skillfully brought his big boat alongside and motored ahead on a parallel course, keeping station about a metre off our port side.

A crewman appeared from a doorway beneath the bridge carrying something that I couldn't see; he leaned over the rail, swung his arms towards me and two large fish landed in the cockpit!

I waved my thanks as they drew away.

Now, I'm OK with cod and chips but otherwise I'm not particularly fond of fish; however, determined to appreciate the fisherman's

generosity, I set to work. The fish, which I think were Sea Bream, were slimy, smelly and tough; I made a bloody mess on the afterdeck, cut my finger and broke the point off the carving knife!

But I did manage to cut some respectable fillets.

Petrels followed our wake, scooping up the bits that I threw overboard.

I sprinkled the fillets with a little pepper, fried them in olive oil, and was pleasantly surprised at their delicious flavour.

Then I had to get rid of the smell from my fingers, the knife, the chopping board and the deck. It wouldn't do to be cutting fillets of fish in an inflatable life-raft.

That night, as we slipped along the coast, we crossed the invisible border: I raised the Uruguayan courtesy flag.

The seaside town of Maldonado was not far off my planned route and the chart showed a yacht club just around the headland; I guessed that there would be fuel there.

When the wind died completely we motored over a glassy sea, close to the shore, past swimmers and beaches dotted with sunbathers. Behind the sandy beaches the sharp, angular tower blocks of Punte Este (East Point) were dark against the early evening sky.

Around the point, five or six yachts were obviously heading for the marina, I followed them in and there, dead ahead, was the fuel jetty. The attendant was about to close up for the night but he waved me in, filled me up, accepted US dollars in payment and then said I could tie up and stay alongside until he opened at eight in the morning. That was a piece of luck.

I had a quick wash, put on some clean trousers and strolled towards the town. What looked like a small ice-cream parlour on the promenade turned out to be an internet café with international telephone facilities, so I called home before wandering on.

I was waylaid by the first café I came to where I sat down and ordered a beer.

I thought about going through the immigration process - for about two seconds - before deciding that none of the offices would be open at half-past-eight in the evening and, with an enforced departure time of something before eight o'clock in the morning, it wasn't worth thinking about.

I sipped the cold beer and watched the sun go down over the Rio de la Plata – The River Plate, but before I'd drunk more than a couple of mouthfuls I found myself nodding off at the table. I abandoned the thought of another beer and wandered back to the boat for a whole night of undisturbed sleep. Big, fat sea lions stretched out on a nearby pontoon snuffled and snored, I probably did too.

We slipped out early in the morning, past long rows of gleaming white powerboats sitting silently on their moorings, heading across the estuary towards Argentina, about a hundred and twenty miles away. All through the day we motored over a flat, grey sea, changing course now and then to avoid large clumps of vegetation that were floating down on the stream.

Towards evening a little breeze blew across the river and we sailed again; but the air was hot, uncomfortable and somehow menacing.

A dark, fuzzy cloud glowing with flashes of lightning filled the horizon ahead; there was no way to avoid it as it rolled across the sea towards us.

I put two reefs in the mainsail and shortened the foresail.

Wham! The wind struck like a hammer.

I wedged myself in the cockpit and sat back to watch the fireworks.

The sky was now black but the brilliance of the flashes left such strong images in my eyes that for a second or two it was impossible to discern which was image and which was real. 'Wind Guru' on the internet had forecast 12 knots of wind for Buenos Aires. Where I was, not so far away, it reached force 9! We managed to steer at about 70 degrees to the wind, climbing obliquely up and over the rapidly building waves.

I dozed off on the leeward cockpit seat with the collar of my foul-weather jacket pulled up tight around my ears to stop my head from lolling about.

The storm passed and left us with no wind at all. On went the engine again: we made about three knots through the water, but what a shock when the GPS showed a speed over the ground of only half a knot! My pilot book shows a half knot contrary current in this area, ours was at least two and a half knots. I did a quick course-to-steer diagram and turned further east.

All night and most of the next day I was kept busy with the changes in wind direction: south-west to north-east then back to north then south-west again; but by the next evening we were reaching along under full sail in the right direction.

I could see Argentina! We closed the coast; it looked very pretty in the evening sunlight, but there was another long, fuzzy, black cloud on the horizon ahead.

I looked up to confirm that the wind was blowing our way but, as if it were power driven, that nasty, glowing cloud ahead was definitely coming directly towards us. Another heavy, hot breeze blew off the land for a few minutes; time to batten down the hatches again. This time two reefs weren't enough. Once more we were struck by a violent wind and the lightning was all around, flickering like a faulty fluorescent tube, but thousands of times brighter. One huge, brilliant flash struck the water close to the boat, the thunder was instant, loud and frightening.

I sat in the companionway admiring the 'Son et Lumière' and wishing it would go away; there was nothing else to do.

The storm did go away and left us with wind from dead ahead. I hove-to and slept for a while. Change came with a suddenness that caught me napping, literally; I woke to find us running before a force 4, with our deep-reefed sails sheeted in hard and the autohelm struggling. I took down the main, poled out the headsail and we made our best 24 hour distance yet: 122M.

There was little change in direction, but towards the next evening the wind strength increased significantly and the waves were building.

Down below, mounted on the forward saloon bulkhead, is a brass bell given to us years ago by some Dutch friends; part of the engraved inscription reads, in Dutch, 'Don't let It Ring' meaning that if it rings it's too rough and we should be tucked up safely in harbour. We were crashing through the waves with just a scrap of foresail flying and the bell had been ringing all afternoon!

Some of the waves were quite spectacular: a beautiful, deep green with tumbling, white crests against a cloudless, blue sky.

I took some photographs. Then one big wave hit the hull with a mighty thump, solid water poured in over the side and filled the cockpit. I was drenched and, sadly, the camera was dead.

By midnight the wind and waves had died too. I ran the engine until a warm breeze blew from the east for a while.

Dawn wasn't welcoming: the sky looked ominous with low clouds glowing like cinders in a fire. The wind drew ahead, gradually increasing in strength until once more we were down to three reefs, crashing into the big waves that were rolling towards us.

The second autohelm gave up the struggle: a minor, maritime disaster, something I would have to fix and I needed to be on shore to do that. The only possibility within two-hundred miles was Puerto Madryn, at the head of Golfo Nuevo, a huge, circular, almost landlocked bay some thirty miles across. The entrance to the bay was twenty-five miles ahead. I didn't know exactly what I would find there, but the word 'Puerto' (port) was encouraging.

On went the engine and I took the helm.

An hour later we'd barely moved despite making at least three knots through the water. I closed the shore to reduce the effect of the current that was obviously holding us back.

Slowly we bashed our way through the waves, past a series of small bays with rocky headlands.

It was getting dark and the wind strength was increasing. Soon the rigging began to moan; the wind generator roared like an aeroplane driving through the sky; sheets of spray, torn from the tops of the waves, lashed against the sprayhood. The luff of the mainsail, which I had wound up hard, curved away from the mast between the slides and I was glad I'd hardened up the topping lift to take some of the strain off the leech. For the first time in years I rigged a clew-earring to reinforce the reefing line.

Each time the bow lifted over a crest, the wind pushed it sideways, it was hard to hold the tiller down and maintain anything like a course. All the time the Yanmar thumped away, giving us steerage; without it we would have had to heave-to or turn and run.

The night passed slowly as we worked our way along the line of cliffs about a mile to leeward. Gradually, as we closed the southern shore of the entrance to the gulf, the seas grew smaller. I rigged 'Moaning Minnie' and took the chance to snatch twenty minutes of badly needed sleep. I'd steered by hand, non-stop - except for one quick 'loo call', for twenty-two hours.

At last, in the lee of the southern shore of the gulf, the sea was smooth again; the wind still roared from over the low hills to the south but the boat was steady and I could make a cup of tea; I needed one.

The cheerful voice of 'Port Control' on the VHF radio saying "come on in" sounded wonderful.

Puerto Madryn doesn't have a sheltered harbour, just two long piers jutting out into the gulf, where large fishing boats and cruise liners tie up.

Close to the northern pier a friendly, fishing boat skipper invited me to tie up alongside.

840 Miles 10 Days

Puerto Madryn to Puerto Deseado

I thought I'd found a perfect berth. I collapsed onto my bunk and slept until, a couple of hours later, big swells began rolling in from the east and shouts from one of the fishing boat crew dragged me back to consciousness.

Despite fenders and a couple of tyres hung over the side by my kindly neighbours, my port navigation light had disintegrated against the steel hull and, the way the wind and seas were building, there was a danger of damage to Cracklin' Rosie's hull. I had to move.

Along the shore, a couple of miles to the south, is an open anchorage. I judged from the wide ribbon of glistening sand I could see beyond the breakers that the tide was low; so I motored in towards the shore, lowered the hook in about five metres of water and let out forty metres of chain. With passport, ship's papers, clean shirt and trousers, some shower-gel all wrapped in a towel and stuffed into a waterproof bag I got ready to row ashore.

Inflating the tender was not easy on the rolling deck and rowing through the tumbling wave crests was exciting; I timed the final approach to coincide with a wave rolling in so that we could surf up onto the sandy beach. The chosen wave approached from behind, I dug in the oars and pulled hard. Not hard enough: the wave rolled underneath the dinghy leaving us wallowing in the trough; the next wave lifted the stern of the dinghy, tipped me out over the bow and deposited us both in a heap on the shore. I was grateful that the water was warm and the sun shining.

Club Nautico Atlantico Sud is almost on the beach; before I'd reached the breakers, Daniel, one of the club staff, had walked down to help me carry the dinghy up to the boat park. Club members made me welcome and there were hot showers!

Refreshed, I walked along the shore-side road to the maritime police station to register my arrival, which was quick and easy in the small, provincial office.

The rising wind veered into the north-east and it was a wet and wild fight to get through the waist-high breakers crashing onto the beach. Rowing back was rough; Cracklin' Rosie was dancing when I reached her.

Back on board I let out the last twenty metres of anchor chain and buoyed it for slipping. There was no room for mistakes in the slanting, onshore wind.

Down below I dried off and climbed into my foul-weather gear.

The rigging began to moan, then howl, then roar as we tossed and pitched. Crests of breaking waves hissed across the deck bursting against the sprayhood.

Hanging on an anchor in 60 knots of wind is uncomfortable, and frightening!

I kept watch through the long night hours, wedged in the companionway, checking our position against street lamps on the shore every minute or so, debating whether or not to slip the anchor chain and head out to sea. But, still tired from lack of sleep, I was reluctant to move, so we hung on.

Slowly the wind backed. Six hours later wind and waves began to subside. Once more I fell onto my bed and slept.

When I woke the sun was shining and the sea was a calm, beautiful, blue; I rowed ashore to have a look around the town.

There were two or three cafés in the row of shops along the seafront, with tables and chairs outside in the sunshine. I took a seat and ordered coffee, comfortably relaxed after the excitement of the last few hours. Quite by chance I got into a conversation with a man at the next table, he was a seafarer too, in fact he turned out to be the captain of the cruise-liner that was berthed on the long pier to the south of where Cracklin' Rosie was anchored. We talked about the previous night's strong winds: he told me that when he'd approached the pier the wind speed had been sixty knots and that his three bow and two stern thrusters had not been powerful enough to get him alongside; he'd had to back off and stay out at sea until the wind dropped.

Four days later my new autohelm arrived, a sturdier model this time (and much more expensive!) with it came a new echo sounder; they both came with Ida. She'd booked her holiday from work and bought a ticket to Ushuaia. But I was in Madryn, about eight-hundred miles too far north, so she got off the 'plane in Buenos Aries. I hired a car and drove the thousand miles to meet her.

There are two terminals in the Buenos Aries international airport. I stood watching streams of passengers disembarking through the gate at terminal A. Ida came out through terminal B.

We drove southwards on long, straight stretches of road, past cattle farms complete with Gauchos on horseback and fields of sunflowers which gradually gave way to scrub covered plains. We exchanged stories of people back home and my adventures on the sea as the miles rolled by.

About half-way back to Puerto Madryn we stopped in Bahia Blanca and booked into a delightful little hotel for the night. A rather handsome restaurant beckoned when we went for an evening stroll; it had a German name but the menu was in Spanish so we struggled a bit and asked the waiter for help; I can't remember the name of what he recommended but it tasted good.

Despite the delicious food and the pleasure and comfort of our hotel I wanted to get going, I was anxious about Cracklin' Rosie lying unattended at anchor; Daniel had promised to keep an eye on her but I knew there would be nothing he could do if she dragged her anchor when the wind blew; there's no way of getting out to the boat once the surf starts to build.

We left early in the morning. Five-hundred miles later we crested the hill overlooking Madryn, and there she was, sitting gently in the sunshine exactly where I left her.

Puerto Madryn and the people who live there are lovely and the beef is delicious: a steak dinner for two, with wine, cost about twelve or fifteen pounds!

Medical care was good too: one side of Ida's face turned a vivid purple one morning when, standing on the cockpit seat, she turned and accidentally poked her head into the wind generator blades; I don't have a 'fridge so there are no packets of frozen peas on Cracklin' Rosie; big waves breaking on the shore meant that first aid was rest and wet towels until the following morning when the wind backed and subsided. We climbed into the dinghy and rowed to the beach; Ida walked the short distance to the local hospital where she was looked after beautifully by a lady doctor who said, surprised at the question, that there was no charge for the treatment.

We spent the days scouring the town for bits of chandlery, working on the boat and enjoying the sunshine. Young sea lions swam alongside for a free meal whenever we ate in the cockpit, and we could photograph them after a couple of long-distance 'phone calls to the insurance company resulted in the purchase of a new camera. I discovered later that whales visit from time to time, although we didn't see any, and there are penguin rookeries all around the shores.

We had some anxious moments too: sometimes we were trapped on board when the waves built quickly making it too dangerous to row ashore, at other times we couldn't get through the surf to get back to the boat. None of the weather sites I looked at in the internet café gave accurate forecasts for the area and it was difficult to predict when the wind would blow hard. Members of the club told me that the winds on the east coast of Argentina had been different that southern summer, alternating north and south on an almost daily basis; I watched the barometer rising and falling and concluded that we were right in the path of a series of depressions - just like home, except that the sun shone most of the time and it was warm.

On shore we stayed in a friendly hotel just off the sea front; I could see Rosie at anchor from a window at the end of the corridor and for the whole of the month that we were there her anchor didn't budge.

Ida stood on the beach and waved when I left. The wind came from the south-east so I took shelter in a nearby bay for a while and cut some more holes in the bulkhead for the new autohelm and echo sounder control units.

Before dawn it was blowing from the north; I hauled in the anchor and headed for the open sea.

By mid-day we'd cleared the gulf and were riding big Atlantic rollers.

I wasn't surprised when the next day brought calm at first, then headwinds. I hove-to. I s'pose I'd given in and decided that sailing fifty miles against a strong wind to gain ten is hard work and not worth the effort.

Sure enough, the next dawn brought back the favourable north wind; once more we were sailing towards The Horn, albeit somewhat sluggishly: there was weed on Rosie's bottom, she needed a scrub.

I'd bought an interesting Argentinian chart in Madryn, it showed a sheltered anchorage about a hundred and thirty-five miles further south, just beyond Cabo Das Bahias – The Cape of Bays - between Isla Leones (Lion Island) and the shore. The forecast and my own predictions were for headwinds again the next day, so I made for the cape.

We crept in to the spot on the chart which showed a sandy bottom. The sun was setting over the mainland hills as I lowered the anchor and the wind was rising again. Comfortably sheltered and safe I slept 'til dawn, then blew up the dinghy and rowed ashore.

Flocks of gulls and terns burst into the sky, screeching at me as I walked up the beach; penguins scurried into their burrows or waddled down to the sea

Higher up, amongst shrubs and prickly cactus, were the remains of an old wooden boat; a little further on a big, rusting anchor lay amongst the rocks; I wondered how they got there, so far above the highest of high tides.

Hiding behind a thorny bush I watched three penguins posing and preening themselves.

Further along the beach a group of sea lions turned to stare as I approached, then lumbered down to the water's edge. I was amazed that such huge animals should be afraid of me.

I stood on the sloping, pebble beach and a thought slowly filtered its way into my consciousness: 'I could get at the weed on Rosie's bottom by careening'. Searching in the clear water for anything that might endanger the boat, I rowed to a spot where we could safely take the ground. On the shore I gathered some large pebbles and built two small cairns - makeshift leading marks to guide me safely in through the rocks.

In the calm of the morning, an hour or so before low tide, I put us aground in my chosen spot. Rosie heeled a little as the last of the tide ebbed away. Chest deep, I scraped, scrubbed, and shivered in the cold water until much of the weed and barnacles were gone, then waded ashore and lay on the sun-heated pebbles to get warm. I was thoroughly cold and it took a while; then I had to wade back through the cold water to get aboard again, I'd left the dinghy tied to the boat!

Cracklin' Rosie straightened herself up as the tide came back in and we headed off towards the south; out past the sea lions that roared as we went by, and across Golfo San Jorge, with a lovely, gentle, following wind filling the sails.

I saw my first albatross, something I'd been really looking forward to, and I wasn't disappointed. Further south I saw hundreds, possibly thousands of them but this one was beautiful, even in this gentle wind he soared, back and forth across the waves making turns so steep that his wing tips almost touched the water; I was so excited I almost forgot to take a picture. I didn't know if it was a he or a she but he - or she - was too beautiful to be an 'it'.

Twenty-four hours later, as the shoreline crept into view above the horizon, the sea turned an undulating, glassy grey.

On went the engine.

The moon that night was a brilliant orange, reflected on the smooth, dark surface of the ocean to the east. Our wake made a silver trail stretching out astern through the still water. There was not another vessel anywhere.

I hoped we'd escaped the area of strong winds blowing from north and south but we were using fuel which meant finding somewhere to buy more. I re-read The South Atlantic Pilot and studied the coastline on the charts again.

Puerto Deseado, five-hundred miles north of The Horn, looked like a possibility and, being on the eastern edge of a large lump of Argentina that juts out into the ocean, was conveniently close to our planned track.

It was late into the next day when I headed in towards the harbour; there was still no wind so pilotage was easy: we motored past rocks I couldn't see, covered at half-tide according to a note on the chart, and between low, rugged cliffs each side of the narrow entrance, until the mast of a sailing boat sticking out above a breakwater on the north bank told me that there might be somewhere for a small boat to tie up or anchor.

We rounded the end of the breakwater. Three small yachts anchored in a tiny bay came into view; I found a space and joined them.

395 Miles 6 Days

Puerto Deseado to Ushuaia

Not far above the beach, at the head of the little bay, is The Fishing and Boating Club Deseado, where visitors are made very welcome - at least I was, so I assume others are too. I hadn't been ashore more than ten minutes before I'd shaken hands with everyone in the clubhouse, been served a drink and begun answering questions about where I came from and how I'd come to be in Deseado. It was most enjoyable, but I didn't last long: two or three beers into the conversation I could feel myself nodding; I think they understood. I said goodnight, rowed back to the boat and slept for about twelve hours.

I didn't have to get dressed when I woke up, I'd fallen asleep in my clothes.

I poked my head out of the hatch, sniffed the sunshine and looked over towards the shore: from the wet pebbles below the high-water weed-line I estimated that the tide was about half-way out. I started the engine, pulled up the anchor and motored towards the club's jetty; I'd been given leave to come alongside to complete the scrub-off I'd half-completed on the beach at Isla Leones.

I didn't quite make it.

I misjudged the slope of the beach and went aground about two metres away from the jetty. Full revs in reverse and she wouldn't budge. Quickly I rowed a line out from the stern and tied it to one of the legs at the seaward end of the jetty, rowed back, climbed aboard and wound the line around a winch, I put the engine in full astern again and winched hard; but it was too late, the water was already well below Cracklin' Rosie's waterline. We were stuck and the tide was falling fast; soon she would start to heel: potential disaster either way.

I grabbed the anchor and a long line (rope) from the cockpit locker, rowed ashore and ran about fifty metres along the beach, carrying the anchor and trailing the line behind me. I dug the anchor into the sand, tied the line to the ring on the end of the shank, rushed back to the boat, joined the line to the end of the spinnaker halyard and winched it in, just in time; she heeled away from the jetty: one danger averted. With one end of a mooring line tied to one of the legs of the jetty and the other end led back to the starboard sheet

78

winch I heaved us back almost upright.

I rigged two more lines between the foot of the mast and the jetty, pulled them tight, then relaxed the line on the winch a little to even up the strain. I took another long line, rowed ashore again and tied the end to a large rock at the water's edge some distance away; back on board I joined the other end to the spare main halyard and wound that in to match the tension in the spinnaker halyard. Now she was secure. My breathing slowed to a rate slightly lower than frantic so I

made a cup of tea and watched the water ebb away; when it was knee deep I climbed over the side and started to scrub. Two people I'd met in the clubhouse the evening before came over for a chat; they congratulated me on the clever way I'd rigged the boat to dry out so that I had easy access all round!

Cracklin' Rosie was clean, refloated and temporarily moored alongside the jetty, I sat in the cockpit and watched a group of youngsters laughing and shouting, kayaking and paddling small dinghies around the bay; they were taking part in a programme of activities designed to teach respect and love for their environment; a scheme run by retired lawyer Carlos Olivia-Day who has himself kayaked around Cape Horn, and more: he'd paid for all the drinks in the yacht club bar on the evening of my arrival, and slipped out of the door before anyone could argue!

With Rosie back at anchor in the bay, I took a taxi into town with my empty fuel cans, filled them with diesel and ferried them back to the boat.

I left early next morning, waving a sad goodbye because the club is a friendly, hospitable place and I would have enjoyed a longer stay.

Hundreds of penguins standing on the south shore of the river watched my departure, one or two of them flapped a wing (or is it a

flipper?) I waved back.

The current carried us out past the half-tide rocks I'd carefully avoided on the way in, and into the swells left over from the previous night's strong wind. We covered a few miles in the puffs and starts that fluttered across the sea before they died away completely, only to be replaced by wind from the south, again.

That wind died with the day and we motored into the night, leaving a brilliant phosphorescent trail streaming aft in the black water.

We were in a high pressure cell. What wind there was came from the south and I set the sails whenever possible. I kept a speed log to see which way the current was carrying us and motored when otherwise we would have gone backwards. Nothing changed until the evening of the third day of high pressure, then the barometer fell, the wind returned and we sailed all through the night.

A glimmer from the afternoon sun struggled through the clouds to briefly lighten the dark hills of Cabo San Vicente, just a few miles from the entrance to The Beagle Channel.

I was excited at the thought of entering the channel, following in the wake of Charles Darwin and Captain FitzRoy on their famous voyage to The Galapagos in HMS Beagle.

With the wind now aft and a favourable current we made six knots over the ground towards Cabo San Diego, the headland that marks the beginning of the channel and the fearsome Estrecho de Le Maire, the fifteen-mile-wide strait between Isla Estados (Staten Island) and Tierra del Fuego.

When a strong wind blows against the tide, standing overfalls in the strait are reported to reach a height of fifteen metres! I didn't fancy that. However, as with the Portland Race, there is an inshore route: by keeping just outside of the kelp fields and inshore of the race local fishermen are said to follow a path of smooth water that runs more or less parallel with the coast. I did the same, albeit with the knowledge that it was neaps and the tide and wind were going my way. There probably weren't any overfalls anyway.

We rounded the cape and turned to the west; clearly we were through and I congratulated myself on having 'done it'.

My mood of self-satisfaction was short lived: movement in the sky caught my eye, I looked up to see great bundles of cloud rolling over the hills and down the valleys to blast out over the sea.

The downdraughts were violent; I kept within a mile of the shore but even so white horses crashed against Rosie's topsides as if we were out in the open ocean.

I put three reefs in the main and turned on the engine.

Ten miles ahead was Bahia Aguirre, the anchorage I'd selected as a stopover. Navigating the Beagle Channel at night is not an easy option especially when the wind is howling, so being windblown, wet and miserable was the only change in my plan.

Three stormy hours later the sail came down and we motored into the almost landlocked north-west corner of the bay; the anchor bit into the sandy bottom, I made some supper, had a tot of medicine and went to sleep.

I woke early and motored out against a gentle breeze towards the channel. Within five minutes the wind speed increased from almost nothing to about force six from the south. I put the helm down, then the anchor, had a cup of tea and went back to sleep.

Slowly the barometer climbed; equally slowly the wind strength decreased. Fleeting patches of sunlight revealed a scene that could have been a loch in Scotland: beautiful, sharply defined hills climbing up to the clouds and firs growing down to the water's edge. I painted all afternoon, and went to bed early.

There was a pale patch in the sky to the east when my alarm buzzed; the hills were still dark. Carefully I followed the route I'd plotted out into the Beagle Channel, and headed west. At five knots, if the wind held and if we could ride two tides, Ushuaia was only a day away.

As daylight filled the sky, clouds rolling over the islands ahead left trails of misty rain, hiding the rugged peaks with their patches of brilliant, white snow.

Soon we were in the shelter of the channel proper; I ticked off the islands and headlands on the chart as we passed. We sailed through the narrows past the rocks off Isla Gable, which must have caused Captain FitzRoy some anxiety, I was grateful to have charts that I could trust.

Further on, in the wider, deeper approaches to Ushuaia, the lights of the world's most southerly town shone invitingly as darkness crept into the day.

There was barely any daylight left when the wind changed abruptly. Short, breaking waves came from dead ahead, slowing us to about three knots. We struggled towards the harbour, with the Yanmar working overtime and spray bursting over the foredeck, until I could slow the engine for the Prefectura Naval (Coastguard) to guide us in to berth alongside a large, Italian boat moored on the yacht club jetty.

We'd reached Ushuaia, only 100M north of Cape Horn.
678 Miles 9 Days

Around The Horn!

Tied up safely alongside in Ushuaia was a good place to be: the wind that had slowed our approach the evening before was now whistling through the rigging, slack halyards were clanging wildly on nearby masts. Outside the harbour the Beagle Channel was white with broken water; but I could step ashore onto the yacht club jetty, take a taxi to town for a few pennies, and the steak was still delicious.

When my friendly Italian neighbours left I moved around to the other side of the jetty and moored alongside Santa Maria, a charter yacht whose Chilean skipper Oswaldo, and Olly, his mate, were hospitable, helpful and generous with information about channels and anchorages amongst the islands.

That night I plotted my route to The Horn.

After clearing with the Prefectura, where I'd been apologetically fined for not clearing properly from Deseado, a mistake easily made when there is a language barrier, I cast off.

Rested, fed, clean, and with a light wind from the west, I sailed back eastwards along the Beagle Channel in warm sunshine, between snow covered peaks in Argentina to the north and Chile on the other side, to the south.

We broad reached the twenty-five miles to Puerto Williams to enter Chile and get clearance for The Horn.

I rafted up amongst a cluster of yachts in a quiet little creek that could have been in the Lake District, and wished I'd had time to stop and paint; but winter was approaching and I wanted to be on my way northwards towards the sunshine before the weather got even worse.

The wind was still in the west, but stronger, when we left in the morning; we raced along under shortened foresail, surfing on the breaking waves; a few inconvenient splashes came aboard as we skirted the shoals and rocky islets.

The Chilean Navy called on the radio to check my identity and confirm that all was well; they keep a tight control of all vessels in the area.

Not far from Puerto Toro, where I'd planned to stop overnight, the wind suddenly died to nothing. My recently gained experience in these waters told me to take in sail; within minutes it proved a good decision: wavelets formed and rapidly developed into breaking crests from dead ahead. I motored upwind for the last mile and anchored off the little fishing village that is one of the original settlements on Tierra del Fuego. Excluding research stations in Antarctica, Puerto Toro is the southernmost permanently inhabited community on the globe; there were thirty-two inhabitants counted in the census of 2002.

The first light of dawn guided me out past the rocks at the head of the bay and the Navy called again. The forecast was for more strong winds from the west, but it was only about force four as we reached southwards across the fifteen miles of open water to the Wollaston group of islands, named around 1830, by a British naval officer, after the English scientist William Hyde Wollaston who was famous in his day for having developed a successful method of processing platinum ore – although I couldn't immediately see what that had to do with a remote island in southern Chile.

The chart tells of a local magnetic anomaly in the bay and there certainly is one! As the autohelm meandered I adjusted and readjusted the sails before realising what was happening; then I used the wind as a directional reference, together with visual transits and a little help from the GPS.

We sailed into a winding channel between steep sided islands. Windswept firs, with white, twisted trunks clung to the lower slopes.

In the shelter of a shallow valley, a two story house stood dark and empty, emphasising the wild loneliness; I wondered who might have lived there and what they'd had to do just to stay alive.

My eyes flicked between the echosounder and the way ahead; here and there jagged lumps of rock, overpopulated with cormorants, protruded above the surface; they stink!

I lowered the anchor to a sandy bottom in Caleta Martial, a delightful little bay on the island of Herschel, and sat in the cockpit with a beer as the sun went down; less than a day's sail away from my goal. A young Herring Gull swam up close to the stern to share my peanuts.

A soft rain fell in the morning, so did the barometer, to 980mb; but the wind was light. The sun broke through the clouds as I motored along the northern shore of the island before turning south and setting the foresail in the gentle, following breeze.

We rolled our way towards The Horn, the sail backing and filling and the mast like an inverted pendulum swinging back and forth.

Not far from the sharp, pointed rocks off the western end of Isla Hornos I looked to the west: huge, dark clouds were billowing over the horizon; it became a race to see if we could beat the weather.

I turned towards the east as a sudden, fierce wind blasted us with hail and rain. A mile or so to the north The Horn disappeared in the grey blanket of falling water; waves built quickly into short, steep breakers that threw us violently left and right. I had to steer by hand again when the autohelm gave up the fight.

Brief shafts of sunshine shone between the racing clouds to illuminate patches of the island hills and the waves crashing against the rocky shore. Icy spray mixed with the rain and hail flew horizontally across the breaking crests as we corkscrewed our way round into the lee of the Island.

We'd rounded The Horn!

Yippee!

But there wasn't much time for celebration: the scrap of foresail I'd set began to shake in the violent wind; I reduced it to a tinier scrap. The Yanmar thumped away and I made for shelter.

At that moment I was worried: continuing to The Falklands in a gale of wind without reliable self-steering was not something I wanted to do. I needed time to think and consider the options; I steered back northwards towards the sheltered channels between the islands.

Six hours later the anchor went down in almost the same spot as the night before and for two days the storm raged around us. We were safe in our little bay with five metres of water under the keel and fifty metres of chain veered, so I changed the engine oil and painted another picture: 'Cape Horn' as I remembered it.

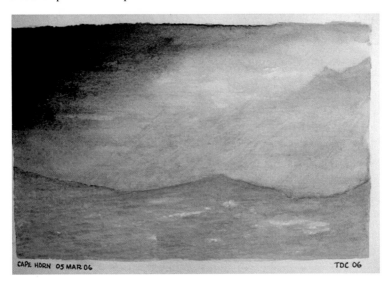

CAPE HORN 05 MAR 06   TDC 06

Occasional lulls raised my hopes but they never lasted for more than a few minutes; the barometer dropped to 970mb.

On the morning it started rising again I left, heading back towards Ushuaia; at least there we'd be in a safe harbour with good communications home. I still wasn't sure of the best course of action.

A few stars shone and the dark shapes of the islands were silhouetted against the sky as we picked our way down the narrow channels. We reached back across Bahia Nassau, past Puerto Toro and back into the Beagle Channel. The wind was good and we averaged 5.8 knots for the seventy miles back to Puerto Williams, I don't think Rosie has ever gone so fast for so long!

I motored slowly into the little creek where yachts moor while they wait to clear into or out from Chile; a friendly wave from a blue and white, steel sloop invited me to tie up alongside. I'd barely finished rigging the mooring lines when Keith, Solquest's skipper, invited me aboard for a beer. Chief mate Maria delivered the beer, introduced herself and told me that supper was nearly ready! "There's plenty" she said, "When we saw you coming in I thought you might be hungry and I cooked a little extra."

We talked about our travels: Keith and Maria were wandering, with no fixed destination, sailing to places that they thought might be interesting. They'd set off from Canada a few months before, stopping here and there on their way south down the west coasts of North and South America. They were enthusiastic about the glaciers they'd seen in branches of the main channel further west. I'm afraid I bored them with my steering problems.

The morning was cold, Rosie's decks were dusted with snow; I slipped the lines and headed for Ushuaia, twenty-five Miles away.

Wind-driven waves were rolling towards us, we could only make three knots. Twenty-five miles is a long way at three knots.

I crossed to the Argentinian side, hugging the coast to gain some shelter from each little headland. My cold, wet fingers fumbled with tight bowlines as I changed the courtesy flag.

The sea gradually became smoother as the sky cleared. Buildings in the town began to take shape and, as if in welcome, a whale blew and flipped its tail at me as we entered the harbour.

225 Miles 8 Days

Ushuaia, Argentina to The Falkland Islands

Racha is the Spanish word for squall; they have them in Ushuaia. The wind screams down the steep mountain slopes, hits the water, blasts across the harbour and churns up waves which slap against the hulls of yachts tied to the jetty; shore lines are stretched tight, wind generators roar and skippers look up anxiously as their boats heel to the wind. The words 'safely tied up in harbour' become more of a question than a statement.

I struggled with the autohelm problem: I considered staying in Ushuaia until a new one could be sent down but that might take weeks or even months; the southern winter was approaching and I didn't want to linger. I decided to head for the Falkland Islands; the autohelm had relented and seemed to be at least partly working again, I was rested and feeling much more confident, and it was only four hundred miles to Port Stanley. With all these westerly winds I could sail, and steer by hand all the way if necessary.

Decision made.

I celebrated with a long 'phone-call home and a steak dinner with a glass of wine or two in town.

I'd planned to leave early, but when I woke at 0430 halyards were clanging, flags were as stiff as boards - and pointing in the wrong direction - so much for the westerly winds. I went back to bed.

Later, when the sun came out, the wind did go round to the west; I paid my bills and cleared to go.

The engine wouldn't start. I checked the fuel, bled the system and still it wouldn't start. Then I noticed the 'throttle' lever return-spring lying on the crankcase in two pieces; that's one spare I didn't have. Carefully I bent the two broken ends into hooks, stretched the coils a little, hooked the two parts together and refitted the spring. It worked, but I'd spent two hours diagnosing the problem and fixing the spring; now it was too late to be able to clear the islands at the eastern end of the Beagle Channel in daylight, so I settled for another comfortable night in harbour. Back to beans and rice for dinner though.

The westerly wind was still blowing in the morning when I left. I called the Prefectura on the VHF radio to report my departure. Back home people wish you a good trip; in southern Argentina they say: 'have a safe trip'!

The hills and mountains caught the slanting rays of the sun as the shadows crept down the slopes; the water was smooth and the Beagle Channel looked lovely. I motor-sailed to make distance, I wanted to be in open water before dark, away from the rocks and islands. Bahia Aguirre with its safe anchorage in the NW corner lay 50 miles ahead, and the strait between Staten Island and Tierra del Fuego, the channel to the open South Atlantic, a little further on.

We cleared the last but one of the islands before evening but a thick, dark bank of cloud hid the setting sun. The wind picked up and came in from the south-west: a cold front approaching. I furled the main and reduced the foresail so that the autohelm could cope with the bigger waves; it was still working.

Freezing rain came with the front; sharp lumps of hail battered the deck, the wind backed to the SSW and rapidly increased to gale force.

My safe anchorage was now almost dead downwind, not good for a night approach.

I carried on.

Sailing through the notorious overfalls in the strait could be dangerous in wind-over-tide conditions and I had no way of knowing which way the tide would be flowing when I got there so I headed due east, on a course that kept us five miles south of Staten Island - which had just become sixty miles of rocky lee-shore.

A bright, full moon shone between the racing clouds, lighting the white crests surging up on the quarter; I ran the engine all through the night to keep water out of the exhaust.

The remnants of the cold front disappeared far ahead as the last of the darkness fled over the western horizon, leaving behind big, white cumulus clouds with their gusty showers, and albatrosses wheeling and diving between the waves.

We cleared the overfalls off Punta San Juan at the eastern end of Staten Island and steered for The Falklands. I slept in short snatches; the waves were kicking the stern around and the wind was piercingly cold.

Slowly, over the next forty-eight hours, the temperature rose, the wind dropped and I began to relax. I hoisted the main again.

The pressure went up, the sky turned blue and the sun shone down on The Sea Lion Islands, a 'welcome sign' off the south coast of East Falkland, about seventy miles from Port Stanley. In the west though, high cirrus cloud was becoming streaky and there was a haze in the air: signs of another depression on the way.

I ran the engine again. With seventy miles to go and plenty of fuel in reserve, I determined to make Port Stanley before the next strong wind attacked us.

Here and there a light glimmered along the eastern shore as darkness came; we turned in towards the land just after midnight. I was watching the echo sounder and following the beam of a sectored light shining down the open anchorage of Port William.

The harbour entrance was still eight miles away and we were motoring directly into the wind so progress was slow.

Then the autohelm began playing tricks again: I selected the 'turn to port by 10°' function. Nothing happened except that a message popped up in the course display window telling me that I was 10° off course to starboard! It continued to steer the course selected but refused to change. I had to switch it off, change course manually then switch it on again. Oh well, we were nearly there.

Gradually the beam from the light grew stronger and the water calmer. I could make out the individual lights in Port Stanley but I couldn't see the two red leading lights to guide me through the entrance; that was because, I learned later, they were changed to green three years before and the information hadn't reached my pilot book; but I worked it all out in the end.

The two green lights led us through 'The Narrows' as the entrance to Stanley Harbour is known; street lamps defined the southern shoreline and I motored slowly west along the waterfront in about four metres of water, looking for somewhere safe to tie up.

Street lights flickered behind the silhouettes of masts protruding above the dark shadow of a building jutting out into the harbour. The wind on the starboard bow was stronger now, pushing us towards the shore. I increased the engine speed a little and edged cautiously towards the big ketch moored on the windward side of the building.

A vacant pontoon beckoned; I steered a little closer through the black water. Just in time I saw the long mooring line stretched from the stern of the ketch to a jetty on the far side of the vacant pontoon, right across my path; not something I wanted to tangle with at 4am on a dark and windy night. Quickly I pushed the helm down and turned away.

Beyond the jetty I could just make out two spherical buoys. I flicked on my torch and shone it on the nearest one: a large letter 'W' told me they were wreck buoys; I didn't want to be there either.

I headed on further down the harbour.

Near the end of the long row of street lamps another shape loomed above the water, like an old, wooden ship, heeling as if aground; and so, later, it turned out to be.

I motored on into the strengthening wind towards the end of the harbour; my anchor bit into the mud just as the wind started to blow hard again. I shut the hatch and climbed into my sleeping bag.

At 10am my VHF calls to the Port Stanley harbour control station 'Fishops' were answered. I was given clearance to anchor closer to the town.

In the grey light of a cloudy day the old wooden ship turned out to be the wreck of 'The Jhelum', a barque built in Liverpool in 1849; she'd spent her working life as a trader until, in the winter of 1870, damaged by storms, she sought shelter in Stanley. She has lain there ever since.

I motored back past the two wreck buoys I'd seen, they mark the remains of the American built 'Charles Cooper', last of the packet ships which used to carry passengers and freight between the Americas and Europe; she grounded there in 1866.

I anchored Cracklin' Rosie near the main part of the town, inflated the dinghy and rowed ashore. In the distance, at the eastern end of the harbour, I could see the elegant lines of a three-masted ship that turned out to be 'The Lady Elizabeth', a steel barque built in Sunderland in 1879; for thirty-four years she'd traded across the seas of the world, but in 1913 she hit a rock in the approaches to Stanley and never left the harbour again.

I tied my inflatable to the pontoon I'd seen in the darkness earlier that morning and clambered ashore; as I stood up there was a loud, unfriendly hiss. I looked around quickly and watched my rapidly deflating dinghy detach itself from the sharp corner of the pontoon's aluminium frame. Another Stanley wreck!

Rain made the steps slippery and the wind slapped waves against the quay. At this time of year depressions track further north, with increasing frequency and with them come the strong winds that The Falklands are renowned for. With winter coming on and problems with the steering gear I felt uncomfortable about continuing northwards.

I found Rosie a snug berth ashore, on a cradle, and put her to bed for a while. Then I bought a return ticket for a flight home.

450 Miles 4 Days

A Month in The Falklands with Cracklin' Rosie

18 November 2006.

There she was, upright in her cradle in Ian Bury's yard, coppercoated bottom spotted with the remains of barnacles I'd scraped off before leaving the previous March; woodwork a bit weathered by sun and rain but otherwise looking good.

I looked around the yard which was, and probably still is, full, in a sort of orderly untidiness, of what most people might call junk. But Ian keeps a remarkably accurate mental catalogue of what's in his yard and makes appropriate selections of suitable bits for use in his business of repairing the boats and small ships which come into Port Stanley, damaged, surprisingly often.

I found a ladder, leant it against the side of the boat and climbed up, putting my trust in the old, grey, timber rungs nailed to the uprights, swung my legs over the guardrail and stepped onto the deck.

The key turned smoothly in the lock; I lifted out the washboards and looked around.

Down below she was dry except where some of my stored tins of fruit had rusted through and leaked their juice into the bilge - pineapple and tomatoes were the worst. Cleaning was going to be a major task. As well as the fruit juice in the bilge, anything that could corrode or gather dust had corroded and gathered dust.

An hour or two into the job I made a mug of coffee and leaned back to contemplate the tasks ahead. Absently, I reached for the mug - and raised an open tin of 'Brasso' to my lips..... I didn't get as far as drinking it but wondered what the consequences might have been.

I serviced the heater: I spent a morning on my hands and knees looking up and sideways at the beast, dismantling, cleaning and reassembling the burner, dropping spanners and nuts and washers and making my right elbow sore where it pressed hard on the floor. Then I broke the fuel feed pipe. Disaster! Summer nights are not warm in The Falklands.

There was a tap on the coachroof and Bob, a local sailor, came aboard for a cup of tea. We discussed the broken fuel pipe; he took it away, fixed it and brought it back again. Wonderful, I had heat again. Saturday came, the day my new batteries, sails and windvane steering gear were due to arrive on the weekly plane from Punta Arenas. They'd all been loaded, personally, by me, into a container in the agent's yard in Southampton and dispatched a month or more before. The 'plane came but my boxes didn't. Too many fare-paying passengers had booked seats so the airline left the freight in Punta Arenas, only five hundred miles away but quite out of reach.

I made expensive 'phone calls and sent pleading emails from a friend's computer; the freight company made promises it couldn't keep and my boxes didn't come the next Saturday either. I was anxious and frustrated but Falkland Islanders just shrugged when I told them. "It happens all the time" they said, "you get used to it."

I didn't have time to get used to it and it made me cross.

I considered sailing over to Punta Arenas, after all it's on the shores of The Straits of Magellan, only five-hundred miles away, but it would have been a racing certainty that the boxes would have been on their way to Port Stanley before I got there.

I did all the preparation jobs I could, then pottered and tinkered. I knew that if the stuff didn't arrive by the next Saturday I would have to fly home again: youngest son John was to marry Nadège in early April and I had to be there.

Saturday came. Three of my four boxes arrived, but there was no sign of the fourth which contained my new mainsail.

I dithered undecidedly all through Sunday and Monday morning until just after lunchtime when I 'phoned the travel agent and booked (and paid for!) a flight home.

Ten minutes later the last box arrived on the back of a Landrover.

But the die was cast. I was faced with a nine thousand mile journey and only a hundred days to do it in; any hiccups and I wouldn't make the wedding.

I drilled holes in the transom and bolted on the mounting-frame for my Neptune windvane steering gear, fitted a few other bits and pieces that had come in the boxes then went to the pub. I caught the 'plane home the next day.

The wedding was in Mauritius; the whole family and lots of friends had a fortnight's holiday on the lovely island, Nadège was a beautiful bride and we all wanted to stay there in the sunshine!

Back in The Falklands Again

12 January 2008

Ian Bury was waiting outside the arrivals hall when I got back to The Falklands; he threw my bag into the back of his Landrover, took me to his home and gave me a room for as long as I wanted. That is fairly typical of the Falkland Islanders' generosity. I had so much friendly help there.

Cracklin' Rosie had slept in her cradle for nearly twenty-two months. I climbed aboard, slid back the hatch and lifted out the wash-boards. My eyes wandered around the familiar cockpit and down into the saloon. The stove needed polishing, as usual; my family, nine-thousand miles away in England, were all a couple of years older than their pictures on the forward saloon bulkhead, and there was someone missing: our new grandchild 'Piper' born to Matt and Kiera after I'd left and yet to be included in the gallery.

I put the kettle on and began writing the 'to do' list.

The mast and boom, wrapped in strips of polythene, were lying on slats of timber nearby, next to the spinnaker pole: not a bad place to start.

Wind whistled across the harbour, biting through my thick sweater; I climbed back up the ladder to get a windproof jacket and made another cup of tea on the way.

Tea finished, I stripped off the polythene wrapping, put the boom on a couple of trestles and began freeing off the fittings; the reefing-line anchor-slides on the underside of the boom didn't slide any more; the boom end fitting was welded to the boom by whatever that stuff is that forms when two dissimilar metals stay in contact in a damp, salty atmosphere for any length of time; I squirted WD40 at them, scraped and hammered for two days before they were all free again.

Long days passed: slowly ticking off the jobs and hiding from the rain squalls that swept across the island.

But it was a real pleasure to go 'home' to a bath in the evenings, although I wasn't very good company: sitting in a comfortable armchair in front of the TV after dinner was a recipe for instant sleep; but the same happened to Ian too, so it didn't matter.

The day came when I found myself walking behind the cradle as my lovely little boat was towed towards the sea.

The big crane on the dockside lowered her into the water and the slings slipped out from under the keel. She was afloat.

The engine fired up straight away. I headed off across the harbour to give us a run and to put some juice back into the batteries. I left her tied up alongside while I went back to the yard to help bring down the mast and spars; not long afterwards she looked like a proper yacht again.

Ahead of us on the dockside was a very pretty aluminium ketch, 'Onrust B', flying the Dutch ensign; Hans, her owner, asked if he could come with me when I set off to test my new sails and the new wind-vane steering. With three reefs and a tiny triangle of foresail unfurled we beat westwards up the long harbour; 'real sailing' Hans called it. He gave me a comprehensive explanation of the various functional options with wind-vane steering gear. I was just pleased that it worked.

Dave Eynon, another friend I'd made on previous visits, invited me to use his berth for a while, it was just opposite the supermarket. Catering for a hundred or more days requires a little preparation so I started to gather the shopping; but before setting off on the long haul north up the two Atlantics, I wanted to explore a little around the islands - and get some practice with the wind-vane steering.

Friendly advice and my own observations told me that a cruise in these waters would probably take at least twice as long as the planned route might suggest; the weather can change with dramatic speed and the wind, from almost any direction, is often very strong; but on the morning I left the forecast was good.

Falkland Islands Tour

Two cormorants twittered farewell as I cast off; they'd built their nest on an old tyre hanging from the end of the jetty – you could call it recycling.

Rosie's bow-wave rippled gently across the still, blue water of the harbour; the coloured roofs of the houses in the little town and the slopes of the hills around reflected the bright, morning sun.

Out in the open waters of Port William there was enough wind to sail. I set the wind-vane and sat back to watch: Cracklin' Rosie responded beautifully to each puff of wind.

A few miles east of Stanley I tacked and turned towards the south to navigate between the rocks off Pembroke Point. Then I gybed – hadn't quite got the hang of the wind-vane control!

Silver and grey dolphins played under the bow as we broad-reached southwards along the coast of East Falkland.

The local radio signal grew weaker as we sailed further from the influence of civilization; the hills abeam to starboard grew hazy in the distance; the line of mountains far astern faded with the radio.

Ahead, on the horizon, I could see a stretch of low-lying land jutting out into the ocean. Just around the headland, tucked into a corner of a wide inlet called Choisieul Sound, is Mare Harbour, a little bit of landlocked sea, where a military jetty serves the islands' airfield five miles to the north. I planned to anchor there for the night.

The wind picked up and veered right round to the west as we approached. I had to beat in through the sound to find the entrance to the harbour but, once in the lee of the land, the waves were gentle - at first.

I crept into a tiny bay sheltered by low, grass covered hills, set the anchor and watched a couple of rocks on the nearby shore for five minutes to see that we weren't dragging.

All night the wind blew hard; the anchor chain was taught and, even though we were less than a hundred metres from the windward shore, small waves were breaking and slapping Rosie's sides as she swung.

Hanging on the anchor in a safe, sheltered anchorage, hiding from the howling wind outside, brings on a comfortable and somehow satisfying feeling. I remember feeling the same when we hid in dens that we'd built in the woods when I was a child.

Not long after dawn I recorded gusts of Force 10 on my hand-held 'windometer', so I was surprised to see a twin engined RIB bouncing across the waves towards us, its bow lifting in the gusts. The bearded driver brought the boat alongside in a burst of spray, I grabbed a line, wrapped it around a cleat and invited him on board.

We shook hands. His face showed amazement and, I'm pleased to say, pleasure when I told him my name; he was Major Richard Patterson, he'd been a student of mine and subsequently an instructor twenty years before! Now he was skippering a British Army adventurous training yacht about to set off on an Antarctic expedition, moored just out of sight a little further into the harbour.

We had a cup of tea and spun a few salty yarns from then and now. Later in the afternoon he came back with an updated forecast and gift of a bottle of something slightly stronger than tea.

Twenty-four hours later the wind dropped a little. I stowed the anchor and steered towards the harbour mouth.

With three reefs in the main I unfurled a few rolls of foresail - too many; I started to wind some back in. The spinnaker halyard wound itself into the rolls of the sail and jammed the whole lot solid. I couldn't budge it one way or the other.

I hauled the mainsail in tight, put the engine in reverse, on tick-over, to keep us from drifting towards the rocks and went up to the foredeck.

Thinking clearly in that narrow, rocky channel with half a genoa flapping wildly about my ears wasn't easy; I spent the next half hour getting hot and sweaty in the bitingly cold wind, unravelling the mess.

When it was done I headed for Seal Cove, only twelve miles distant but far enough in the late afternoon and a little further on my way.

I thought there might have been seals in Seal Cove, there weren't, none that I could see anyway. But there was kelp, in abundance. I'd seen small patches of the weed floating far out at sea, and more when we'd followed the edge of kelp fields into the Beagle Channel, but here it was dense: great bundles of long, wriggly, black tendrils snaking across the surface, thick, dark clusters below.

The pilot book states with authority that it's easy to follow a narrow path of clear water through to a sandy patch near the head of the cove; maybe it is on a sunny day, in a gentle wind. My first attempt at anchoring had us drifting towards the nearby shore with about half a ton of kelp on the hook.

But there is a sandy patch and I did find it.

The morning was beautiful: dolphins played around the bow as we headed out towards the sun, gulls walked on the dense patches of weed, and pilotage was as easy as the book had said.

We sailed south in the sunshine, towards Fanny Cove Creek, forty miles away in the Bay of Harbours; I'd read that a Gentoo Penguin rookery of over two million birds stretches along the coast there.

A forest of kelp guards the entrance to the creek and, as the depth reduces, staying on the winding path through the dense weed becomes critical; GPS and charts are not much help, the navigator's eyes are the only reliable instrument; it would be difficult at night.

We meandered cautiously along the ribbon of clear water for a couple of miles and anchored in four metres over thick, black but beautifully safe mud. To the north dark cliffs shielded me from the wind; low, barren hills rolled away to the south. I lit the stove and the oil lamp and relaxed in the warm glow as darkness fell.

A low mist filled our little world at dawn. Two Seals poked their heads above the water to snort a greeting; little, brown Tussock Birds strutted about chattering; they left their calling cards all over my new spray hood. But I didn't see any penguins.

I picked my way carefully through the mist and the kelp and motored gently out to sea. The engine note changed as the propeller chewed its way through individual strands of weed which were almost impossible to avoid and I worried about the self-steering blade.

By the time we cleared the creek the sun had pierced through the mist, the sea sparkled and a little breeze freshened the air; we reached across the wide bay towards the south-east corner of East Falkland, where the fields of kelp stretch out from the land for more than a mile.

Keeping well to seaward we rounded the headland making a gradual turn onto a north-westerly heading into The Eagle Passage.

With wind and tide from astern we raced between the low headlands and islands, past Halfway Cove with its tiny hamlet tucked inside the hook of the headland, along the northern edge of Stinker Island - so called because thousands of Giant Petrels nest there and it stinks – and out into the Falkland Sound.

I headed up-tide and upwind a little so as not to be swept past Fox Bay on West Falkland - on the other side of the sound.

Two hills, dark against the sky, mark the entrance to the bay which is wide open to wind from any southerly direction. Tucked up in the far corner is a sheltered creek that meanders around a headland to a government jetty which serves the village of Fox Bay East.

Across the water, on the far side of the creek, the three or four houses of Fox Bay West looked lonely against the low, treeless hills.

A pair of black and white Harbour Dolphins swam alongside, puffing noisily, as we approached the jetty; people came down to take my lines; they don't get a lot of visitors. Gavin Marsh, the government rep, asked me a couple of official questions then invited me up to his house for coffee, which magically turned into a delicious steak dinner with blackberry tart and custard for desert - what a treat. Conversation meandered from sheep shearing to government defence policy, the weather, daughter Rachel's distance-learning education on a computer constrained by the local dial-up connection system and the harbour Dolphins, known locally as 'Puffin(g) Pigs'.

Comfortably full I wandered back to my little boat tied safely to the jetty and slept. When the sun came up I set off over the grassy hills in search of another penguin colony I'd been told about. I found minefields left over from the 1982 conflict, gulls and buzzards soaring on the air rising over the low cliffs, a pair of Grebes swimming and a Bittern with a fish in its beak; it was a delightful walk but I didn't find any penguins.

Heading north through the sound I looked up at the banks of fluffy cumulus clouds casting shadows over the land on either side, yet we sailed down a channel of sunlit, blue water. But there was a penalty: eventually the wind gave up.

I was beginning to feel the urge to get going on the long trip home;

Stanley was still at least two days sailing away so I decided to continue north while the sunshine lasted: past Port Howard and Many Branch Harbour and into San Carlos Water, scene of so much tragedy during The Falklands War, but now a delightfully safe haven

A flock of fluttering terns turned golden in the evening sun as we rounded a rocky headland into the long inlet.

Motoring eastwards towards the dark, night sky I saw that the steaming light wasn't working. Oh well, there was no one around to see; I turned on the deck light as a substitute.

The high jetty in Port San Carlos made a comfortable, sheltered berth and I could sleep soundly whilst the rising wind scurried down the valleys and around the stunted trees.

In the morning, when I climbed up onto the jetty, I noticed that the steaming light was level with my head; I climbed down onto the boat again, switched on the navigation lights, grabbed a screwdriver and a spare bulb and, with one fall of the spinnaker halyard in my hand, climbed back up. I was about to haul the mast over to unscrew the fitting; when I looked up the light was on!

All that day, and the next, the wind was strong from the north, too strong to set sail if there was a choice. My time was slipping away.

I did some maintenance. One of my cockpit cushions, essential for keeping watch at sea in comfort, had come unstitched along a seam.

Back in Stanley, sewing in a sail batten, my last thimble had slipped off my finger, bounced off the coachroof and tumbled its way over the side; there is though, a haberdashery in the town, open on Saturday afternoons only. I'd made contact by telephone and was told to make an appointment for a fitting, awfully grand for a humble thimble. I attended at the appointed hour. They didn't have my size. I sewed my cushion using a stiff, unwieldy sailmaker's palm.

A friendly farmer picked up the next day's forecast for me: 'strong westerly going north' - we could cope with that.

Light was just creeping into the sky when I cast off. The hills and the water beneath the rising sun were beautiful.

But our initial course was straight into the wind. We struggled through the waves until I could raise some sail and bear away northwards; then we raced along, clearing the high cliffs of Fanning

Head, across the bay towards Dolphin Point.

I tried to cut inside the overfalls off the point, but it was rough with steep waves coming from every direction.

The self-steering had problems: it didn't like the irregular sea and the wind coming from astern. I needed to get rid of the mainsail, difficult on my own in strong winds: I sheeted the foresail in hard and tied the tiller down, that way we lay broadside to the wind and waves. With the mainsheet slack the boom swung back and forth across the coachroof; I clung to the mast with one hand and pulled down the sail with the other, then went back to the cockpit and tightened the sheet; that steadied the boat a little. But we were still on the edge of the overfalls: big, steep waves throwing us all over the place. I steered by hand for a while, until the wave pattern became more regular and I could hand over to the wind vane.

More comfortable now, despite the tumbling waves, I clambered back on deck to tidy up the sail.

Once clear of the overfalls and with a following wind the ride was much less bumpy; it was interesting too: albatrosses performed aerobatics, geese paddled away furiously at our approach; ever inquisitive Rock Shags dived and flapped around us as we surfed along the northern shores of East Falkland.

Towards the end of the day, as we turned south, the blue sky behind the hills turned to gold and the sea became smooth enough for me to enjoy a cup of tea.

The light on Mengeary Point should have guided me past that rocky headland but there was only darkness; I kept well to seaward until the Cape Pembroke light blinked into view. We turned west, into the wind again; once more the engine did the work.

I stared through the spray, searching for the sectored light that had guided me into the deep, wide inlet two years before. Slowly I began to recognise the lights of three large fishing boats at anchor in exactly the right position to obscure the sectored light.

Skirting the fishing boats, I lined up the two green lights which guided us through The Narrows into Stanley Harbour and motored across to the sheltered berth I'd left ten days before.

Two days later Dave Eynon took me out in his motor boat to see some penguins!

285 Miles 9 Days

The Falkland Islands to Salvador, Brazil

The strong south-westerly eased and backed into the south, sunlight glittered on the water; it looked like a good day to go.

Friends slipped the eight the mooring lines I'd rigged as insurance against the storms that sometimes blast through Stanley Harbour.

The brightly coloured roofs of the town looked charming when I looked back to wave. Part of me didn't want to go. I loved The Falklands with their dark, rolling hills rising from a sea that sparkles silver-bright when the sun shines. I loved the people I met who were friendly, and generous with their help. I felt safe there.

Out at sea there was a long swell from the north, short, sloppy waves from the south-west and now the southerly wind was making a new pattern, but with my new wind-vane self-steering, full mainsail and genoa we made a steady four knots until evening when the sky turned a beautiful purple and the wind died completely.

We were totally becalmed. 'Never mind' I thought, 'the wind blows almost constantly in The Falklands, it'll be back soon.'

The sails slatted back and forth. We rolled from side to side in the swells until I could stand the slapping and banging no more. I furled the genoa and lowered the main.

My resolve not to start the engine lasted about thirty minutes, but with such a long journey ahead and no garages on the way I didn't dare run it for more than an hour.

All night we pitched and rolled under the clearest, most beautiful night sky I have ever seen: the moon shone like a lantern and stars down near the horizon were so bright that they could have been the lights of ships; but it was cold, so cold that I went below and lit the heater, something I rarely do at sea, mostly because it means taking the chimney cover off and I don't trust myself to remember to put it back on again.

Slowly the waves settled into a more regular pattern. A light breeze from the west encouraged me to pole out the genoa. We were moving, just, heading for Tristan da Cunha, a tiny island, two thousand miles away. With a population of two hundred and seventy-five, it is the most remote permanent settlement in the world, about fifteen hundred nautical miles west of South Africa, the nearest land.

The wind blows that way most of the time - except that when I wanted to go there it didn't.

The great circle route from The Falklands to Tristan is initially about 070°; I was very tempted to abandon that part of my plan and steer a more northerly course towards warmer waters, but it wouldn't have got us far, the wind died again. I furled the sail.

I ran the engine until the tiniest of breezes ruffled the surface; it didn't seem worth setting a sail again but a check of the GPS showed that without the engine we were making 0.7 of a knot backwards. That was the South Atlantic Current at work, so I set the foresail; it flapped and fluttered all night but our position in the morning showed that in about eight hours we had made a mile of progress; it could have been five miles backwards.

Brilliant, vivid colours of the sunrise were reflected in the gently undulating surface of the ocean, it was like a scene from a fantasy.

Two albatrosses landed not far to starboard; it was fun to see them crook their long wings and push their webbed feet forward to ski along the water before settling.

That evening the sun set in a lovely, golden glow: beautiful; but the sea was still smooth, with long, gentle swells from the south-west and not a flicker of wind.

The weather pattern was set. For days we made very slow progress:

tacking, poling out the genoa, sheeting in, sheeting out and not getting very far.

Then came the fog. I hadn't expected fog: great, dark patches all around and still no wind. After three miserably grey, slightly anxious days the sun finally broke through. Then it was hot!

I hung my 'thermals' in the rigging, they were beginning to smell and I couldn't afford the fresh water to wash them. My black, long-sleeved vest looked like Dracula flying in from astern!

I plotted our track on the chart. We'd been drifting north-west, which was not where I wanted to go. It was time for a decision: we'd made such poor progress – three-hundred and fifty miles in ten days - that I felt uncomfortable about pressing on towards Tristan. I decided to head further north and aim for Ascension Island, which had been an option in my plan and my next port of call after Tristan anyway. Not only that, we'd be warmer sooner!

As if my decision had prompted a change, dark clouds began to gather on the horizon. Wind came in from the north-east and soon I was reefing the mainsail. By 0400 I'd put in the third reef, an unpleasant job in rough seas especially at night.

When the grey light of dawn filled the sky I made a cup of tea: I put it down on the gimballed stove and immediately we were struck by a big breaker; my tea threw itself all over the stove and the galley floor.

That was a decision point too: The barometer was dropping quickly and the wind direction wasn't changing: a depression was heading straight for us. I hove-to on port tack.

All day long the wind strength increased; with the low, dense cloud above, darkness came early.

The night was miserably long, cold, wet and uncomfortable until just before dawn when the cold front passed: suddenly the wind backed and we were sailing fast in almost the right direction. I took off my foul weather jacket and made some breakfast.

Then I made a serious error of judgement: I stepped into the cockpit to adjust the self-steering vane, no more than ten seconds' work. Not one but two waves swamped the cockpit in that ten seconds; I felt a spurt of water pour down my back, through my underpants, down my legs and into my boots.

But we were on course, sailing fast for the first time in ten days. Fluffy, 'trade wind type' cumulus took over the sky.

We rolled and bashed our way through the waves; it was almost as if the south east trade winds had stretched across to the western side of the South Atlantic, lulling me into thinking that all was well.

Then the sea got me again: it was lunchtime; I'd laid out three crispbreads on the worktop (which is actually the engine cover), I had a jar of spread in one hand, a loaded knife in the other and the wave pattern, which had been regular all morning, suddenly featured a rogue which lifted the bow high out of the water, then dropped it sideways into the next trough. Thud! I felt it coming.

Holding on to the knife and the jar of spread I took the shock with my left shoulder against the half-bulkhead at the forward end of the chart table, the dollop of spread flew off the knife and splattered all over the plastic chart cover and me, it's amazing how far a dollop of spread will spread! My right elbow crunched into the crispbreads: the biscuits were totally demolished; the jar was undamaged but upside down on the floor - empty, and my sweater was indelibly stained. I didn't record my comments.

After that it was the albatross: I saw it approaching, some distance away off the port quarter: 'might be a good shot' I thought 'but it'll probably do one of those magnificent wing-tip turns and soar off downwind.' As it grew closer I could see that it was a Black-Browed Albatross, and a magnificent specimen. He got closer and closer until, about seven or eight metres off the stern, he lowered his undercarriage and settled gently onto the water.

He knew my camera was down below.

It was a rocky, rolly night again: anything that could bang or clatter banged and clattered; I was glad I'd taken down the mainsail, which I did in the middle of the night, by starlight. There was no moon but the stars were so bright that the Milky Way looked like a delicate, white cloud stretching from horizon to horizon.

My chocolate store was running low; I only ate one square at a time but sometimes it seemed such a long time 'til my next ration was due that I cheated.

We'd been sailing for thirteen days; I hadn't seen another craft, aeroplane, or much in the way of marine life when splashes on the tops of distant waves caught my eye. Within a few minutes twelve or fifteen small whales (small for whales that is) surrounded us; they were three or four metres long with very blunt noses, shiny black on top and grey underneath; one of them came quite close as if he'd been sent to investigate. Some swam on their backs for a short while, and slapped their tails on the water; they played around us for about fifteen minutes. I waved when they wagged their tails and sped off towards the east.

My 'trade wind' disappeared. Once more we were lurching about in almost no wind at all: slow progress.

Seventeen days out and I saw a ship! I could read a name on the side so I called her on the VHF radio: "Morning Cornet, Morning Cornet, this is Cracklin' Rosie, Cracklin' Rosie, over." The captain kindly reported my position home via email: 38° 39'.9S 39° 17'.7W.

At last the temperature was rising; so was the wind. I'd put in the third reef and was quietly worrying about the strange clouds above: one looked like a long, white fox tail stretched right across the sky.

I hove-to and made a request to Neptune that he might iron the surface of his domain more often.

I did a little maintenance - not easy in a rolling sea but I could manage whipping the ends of the self-steering lanyards.

Whipping finished, I stepped back, literally, to admire my handiwork; my heel landed on the corner of the sewing box: I caught one reel of twine as it flew past my ear but the rest of the contents were strewn all over the place; I spent a while on my hands and knees picking up the needles from between the cockpit floorboards.

For three more days it was rough, but we did make some northward progress. I hate going backwards.

By now we were well to the west of our desired track, 32° 27'.4S 32° 11'.7W to be precise, about 800M out into the South Atlantic. I gave in to the instinct which had been nagging at me since I cast off: 'we'll head north, for Salvador and the sunshine.'

Neptune must have heard and sympathised: by nightfall we were reaching at six knots heading just west of north.

Apart from Cracklin' Rosie and me, the surface of the sea was empty; the only sign of life was dead: a poor little flying fish that must have landed on deck during the night.

Gradually the water turned to that deep, tropical blue where the temperature confirms the latitude and the sun dries out anything that is not kept wet or lubricated. The steering lanyard pulley blocks were squealing like tortured mice; I tried lubricating them with engine oil, WD40, even butter, which was liquid now anyway, but still they went on squeaking.

Peeling off my many layers of clothing was smelly, but what a pleasure!

Five-hundred miles south-east of Salvador I put it all back on again: I was dozing in the cockpit when a couple of raindrops interrupted my snooze; before I could reach the companionway we were in dense, dark rain so intense that I could see nothing; I was soaked in an instant. The wind strength quickly increased to gale force – in an area where there aren't supposed to be any gales! All day I struggled to make some distance in the right direction then, as quickly as it had arrived, the wind veered and fell away to a steady breeze; we made four knots all through the night.

Now we really were in the tropics: by day we sailed in the sunshine; at night the dark sky glistened with millions of stars. Occasionally I had to shorten sail and once I watched a waterspout hanging down from a big, grey cloud, but mostly we reached along in a steady south-easterly.

Two days south of Salvador the sea was no longer empty: I saw five ships, five aeroplanes, dolphins, birds and the occasional plastic bottle floating by. The coast, although not yet in sight, was only thirty-five miles away, almost within swimming distance.

We sailed into Bahia Marina, Salvador, thirty-five days after leaving The Falkland Islands. I tied up to a pontoon, in an ultra-modern marina on the banks of an ancient harbour.

2853 Miles 35 Days

Salvador to Recife

My telephone call home surprised Ida who'd been waiting for a call from Tristan or Ascension: "What are you doing in Salvador?" she asked, as did everyone who had been following my progress. It was good to talk and she told me how the email from the captain of Morning Cornet had prompted a few questions about the accuracy of my navigation.

It was a delicious luxury to take a shower, put on some clean clothes and fall asleep without setting the alarm. I woke in the early evening, walked ashore and sat at a table on the balcony of the marina restaurant; looking out over the moored yachts to the bay beyond I thought about the contrast between now and a few hours ago and how much difference the wind-vane steering had made: we'd sailed non-stop for nearly three thousand miles without the whining of the electronic steering unit and the need to run the engine to keep the batteries topped up.

A helpful taxi driver shepherded me around the tortuous immigration circuit. We swept along a fast, modern carriageway through a forest of skyscrapers, wound our way along the shore through narrow streets lined with fishermen's cottages and searched for offices buried amidst dockside warehouses. Once again people were friendly and helpful but once again the offices opened at different times and seemed to be totally unconnected with each other. But we did it; I could stroll into town without fear of being arrested as an illegal immigrant. If there's a next time I'll stay longer and explore a bit more of the city and the numerous inlets and creeks around Baia de Todos os Santos (Bay of All Saints), the huge bay on which Salvador lies.

The evening before I left I motored round to the fuelling dock and filled up all my cans; then I took a ride to the nearest supermarket to buy some kitchen towel; I found a special offer: 40% more for about the same price as other, smaller packs; I got back to the boat and opened up my bargain. I'd bought thirty-two toilet rolls!

That night it was so hot that I slept outside in the cockpit – until about three o'clock in the morning when it poured with rain: I scurried into the saloon. At least the rain cooled things down a bit so that, after pulling on a dry T shirt and shorts, I could sleep down below for a couple of hours.

Local fishermen were already at sea when I cast off at first light, their patched sails driving their little boats through the swells. Again I marvelled at their casual bravery, sailing out into the ocean in tiny, open boats with no visible safety gear, the way, I guess, that fishermen have done for thousands of years.

The wind was blowing straight into the harbour, pushing back the ebbing tide and making the sea uncomfortable until one of the huge, black clouds drifting overhead released its reservoir and flattened the waves. I have foul-weather clothing; those fishermen would have been soaked.

Outside of the harbour we turned northwards so the wind direction became more favourable: we fine-reached along the coast, past mile upon mile of high-rise buildings, until we could bear away on a direct course for Recife, about four hundred miles further north.

All day we sailed in the sunshine over a beautifully blue sea; I waved to the fishermen as we passed and mostly they waved back; they'd be dry again now.

At dusk the wind dropped away to nothing. The fishing boats turned on their bright, white lights to attract the fish and I turned on the engine. I had to stay alert and change course now and then, there were so many lights bobbing about and it was difficult to judge how near or far away they were. I didn't see any with normal navigation lights; I kept a sharp look-out all through the night in fear of meeting one with no lights at all.

By sunrise they'd all gone home, but the wind didn't come back.

Beyond the horizon the shoreline curved away towards the west forming a long, shallow bay towards Recife. I wondered if there might have been a sea breeze closer to the shore; on the other hand, the Brazil Current is said to run more southerly closer in; I'll never know.

Great, towering clouds rose from the sea all around us, like gigantic columns holding up the sky, with dense, black rain falling beneath them; they were harmless though, they brought a little breeze as they approached but, after washing down the decks, their shadows slowly moved away leaving us to an empty ocean and the burning sun.

We motored steadily over a glassy sea until a change in the engine note worried me out of an after-dinner nap; our speed quickly dropped to about one knot. I looked over the stern: there was half a palm tree trailing behind! An evening breeze was developing and night was coming on; I didn't dare go over the side. I poked at the foliage with the boathook and managed to clear most of it. I checked the self-steering blade and motored ahead; all seemed well and gradually I relaxed. Recife was only sixty-five miles further ahead. The breeze didn't come to much so we motored on through the night.

Sharp white in the morning sun the city tower blocks climbed into view. Soon I could make out the long reef and the harbour wall; this time the entrance was obvious. We swung around the end of the reef, leaving the green-painted lighthouse to port, and picked up a buoy off the Pernambuco Yacht Club. I inflated the dinghy and rowed ashore.

375 Miles 4 Days

Recife to Noronha

The familiar face of Negu, who'd helped me 'immigrate' on my previous visit, appeared when I walked up the jetty; he did it again: we started the next morning, this time it took only a day and a half; not so profitable for the ferryman but I was pleased to get it over and done with.

A little way upstream a catamaran called 'Graffiti' swung at anchor; I'd met the skipper, Chris, on the evening of my arrival; he'd given me an open invitation to coffee any morning around ten. I climbed into my dinghy and rowed over. Sounds of a violin drowned out my knock on the hull; I knocked a little louder. Chris poked his head out of the companionway, waved a greeting and disappeared below again. I wrapped the dinghy painter around a cleat and stepped up onto the spacious after-deck. More music and the smell of coffee wafted up from below; I knew the coffee would be good and he was obviously a very competent musician: in the short time I knew him I heard him play an electric keyboard, a clarinet and a violin.

"Europe" was his answer when I asked where he came from, but home was on his boat; he was meandering around the world, funding his sailing by playing in hotels wherever he stopped for a while. He asked if I played an instrument; I admitted to having a harmonica on board; I also admitted to not being able to play it very well.

"How often do you practice?" he asked.

"About twenty minutes a day" I said.

He was too polite to be rude but he made it clear that three hours a day was the minimum if I wanted to be any good. I changed the subject.

Deep in the depths of his catamaran he found me some two-pot rubber solution; I took my tender ashore, removed the leaking patch that I'd put on in Port Stanley two years before, cleaned up the area and stuck on a new one, all of which takes only a minute to write; cleaning off the old glue and applying the patch took hours; but it worked.

Not far from the clubhouse a convenient concrete wall slopes down into the water. At high tide one morning I leant Cracklin' Rosie against the wall to dry out so that I could check the stern gear: none of it seemed to have suffered from towing a chunk of palm tree.

That evening I had a meal with Chris on the club verandah overlooking the harbour; we watched two young lads casting circular nets from the stern of a small, wooden boat. I was surprised at the amount of fish they pulled in.

There were a few empty beer bottles on the rough, wooden table when we paid the bill; I said 'farewell', I'd been in Recife for a week.

Chris was still asleep when I left in the morning.

A couple of lads in two local fishing dinghies thumbed a tow down the harbour, grinning as they passed me their tow-lines; there was no wind so I saved them a long row and it was fun; they waved a 'thank-you' as I motored out into the swells.

The sails and the wind-vane steering went back to work, on a course of about 030°, aiming for Fernando de Noronha, three-hundred miles north-east of mainland Brazil. We meandered a bit: I wrote 029° in the log, five minutes later it was 035°, even so I was confident that we'd get there, fairly quickly too I hoped - we made six knots all day; but the wind went down with the sun and big clouds filled the sky, brilliant white where the moon shone on them from above, dark, menacing and full of rain below. Ahead of the rain came a brief wind then, after the cloud had passed, flat calm and perspiration heat, as if the cloud had sucked up all the air.

I spent the days chasing the little patches of darker water, where puffs of wind ruffled the surface. At night we just wallowed.

But we got there.

A strong current eddied around the western end of the island, more powerful than the little flurries of breeze. The wind-vane steering was defeated so I rigged the electronic unit and motored along the northern coast towards Porto Santo Antonio five miles further east.

There's no space for visiting boats in the little harbour so I cruised around amongst fishing boats swinging on permanent moorings, looking for a suitable spot in which anchor. We ended up about three-quarters of a mile from the shore, to seaward of the fishing boats; it wasn't an ideal location 'but at least' I thought, 'we should be out of mosquito range'. Not a chance: first it was 'the midnight fliers' then 'the dawn patrol'. To say I was irritated would be putting it mildly; however, tucked away in the bottom of a cupboard I have some ancient, 'army-issue' insect repellent which would probably fail modern health and safety regulations; it smells a bit but it works so I did get a couple of hours undisturbed sleep.

Before making an expedition to the shore, I studied what I could see of the island through binoculars; it is beautiful: green, undulating hills with here and there a patch of grey volcanic rock pushing up through the trees which grow right down to the white-sand beaches.

Just before I launched the dinghy a rank of dolphins swam past, leaping and diving, and making my morning feel good.

309m 3 Days

Noronha, Brazil to Horta, Faial, The Azores

I rowed between the fishing boats towards the tiny harbour to 'phone home and register my arrival with the authorities. All the formalities, I was informed, could be completed in one visit to the Port Captain, whose office, just above the harbour, was shut.

I sat and drank a cup of coffee in a beach cafe then wandered along the row of three souvenir shops. Staff from the shops were sitting on a wall at the end of the row chatting; there weren't any customers; they probably recognized that I wasn't there to buy souvenirs, but they were friendly and helpful when I asked about the harbour office and how I might 'phone home; one of them took me into his shop, dialled the number, then waved away my attempts to pay for the call.

The Port Captain arrived: he was a short man in a white shirt, wearing a peaked cap and a big, welcoming smile; he shook my hand, invited me to sit in the chair in front of his desk and gave me a cup of really good coffee. He talked for a while about his beautiful island and then calculated the charge for my stay, at anchor, about three-quarters of a mile outside the harbour: the equivalent of £45 per day! I was shocked. I didn't have that much in Brazilian Reals so he chauffeured me to the tiny, island airport, about ten minutes' drive away, to get the money from a cash machine. I hate being ripped off so I decided to leave the next day and grudgingly paid the £90.

I climbed into my dinghy to row back to the boat feeling sad. Just then the beaked head of a turtle broke the surface of the water; he turned towards me and stared for a moment before resuming his leisurely swim; that cheered me up a bit.

For my second and last night in Noronha I sailed a little way along the coast towards the west where there is a delightful bay, between two rocky headlands, with white-sand beaches and dense, green foliage climbing the hills behind. I anchored there in 15m, stripped off and dived over the side into water so clear that I could see my anchor chain on the bottom all the way to the anchor!

Over in the eastern corner of the bay people sat around tables on the patio of a beach café, enjoying a drink in the shade of brightly coloured sun umbrellas which fluttered attractively in the cooling breeze. I was tempted; I wrapped my camera and my wallet in a waterproof bag and climbed into the inflatable dinghy.

Surf was breaking heavily on the sandy beach but the corner of the bay was sheltered by a rocky promontory, the breakers there looked no more than knee high.

Approaching the shore I could feel the dinghy rising and falling on the swells; the closer I got the steeper they grew. Not far from the line of breakers a wave lifted me high in the air and as we dropped into the following trough the dinghy bent almost double, with me in the middle! I spun round, headed back seawards and had a beer on the boat. I fell asleep listening to the distant roar of surf pounding on Conceicao beach, about a cable inshore from where we were anchored.

My alarm was the morning sun shining in through the windows; I jumped up, put the kettle on then climbed onto the coachroof and dived into the cool, clear water for a swim before setting off on the long trek to the Azores two thousand five hundred miles to the north.

I would have loved to have stayed longer and explored the island but the heavy charges imposed on visiting yachts made me feel very uncomfortable; I suppose the logic, as it is in many parts of the world, is that if you own a yacht you must be wealthy.

Back on board I made a cup of tea, pulled up the anchor and set sail - only two-hundred and thirty miles to the Equator.

The day grew hot as the sun rose higher in the sky and the wind was light and fickle; with a couple of thousand miles to go I was reluctant to start the engine, but I did when a two-knot current started pushing us back towards the island; the ocean swells were smooth and gentle but I could see the bubbling surf where they surged amongst the rocks at the eastern end of the island. It was slightly worrying to think about the possibility of drifting that way if the engine should fail, but it didn't; I turned it off again when our speed over the ground showed that we'd cleared the current.

Navigating these waters in the days of sail must have been difficult. Great, towering rain clouds threatened strong winds, but they gave just a few little puffs as they passed and left nothing but hot, windless air behind. We rolled and wallowed in the calms, sails slatting back and forth driving me to turn on the engine again and again to motor across the oily sea to the shadow of the next cloud with its little patch of wind. There was a small consolation though: I took a shower in a heavy rain squall to wash off the salt from the morning swim.

After struggling for five days to get there, we crossed Equator in the dark; I'd run out of whisky so I toasted Neptune with a beer. Then, watching the latitude on the GPS flick from south to north and north to south again, I tacked back and forth over the line so that I can say I've crossed the Equator half-a-dozen times in a small boat.

There was still a few thousand miles to go but we were half-way home.

At dawn I watched a shoal of little green fish swimming alongside; we were sailing at half a knot so it wasn't difficult for them to keep up.

The wind and the engine took turns to drive the boat. I motored at little more than tick-over speed, that way we made about three knots but only used half a litre of fuel an hour.

Long, sunny days passed with no ships, no birds and not much visible marine life. There was a brief moment of excitement one morning when two flying fish leapt from the water, flew straight towards each other and almost collided in mid-air! I wondered how much activity there might be under the surface. I thought we were in for another blow when big, dark clouds began to line up on the eastern horizon; they drifted slowly overhead then faded away to the west; rows of fluffy white ones scuttled across the sky to take their place; a little bit of their wind reached down to the sea and gave us a gentle shove, but it didn't last. We didn't do much scuttling.

It was hot; too hot for socks, and my feet had turned blue, not from some rare, tropical affliction but the dye from my sailing shoes; it had happened once before back home: I'd had a little grumble to the company I'd bought the shoes from, they had apologised and sent me a new pair. I thought maybe this might be a way of keeping myself in free sailing shoes; then I decided that I didn't want permanently blue feet so I washed off the dye and put on a different pair of shoes.

Ten degrees - six hundred miles - north of the Equator a ship steamed across our wake; I could read the name 'Samsara' on her stern. I called on the radio and the skipper kindly emailed my position and a message home.

That night I could see the North Star; it should have been visible days before but haze and cloud on the horizon had kept it hidden. It was strange to see the star so low in the sky; I hadn't thought much about it on my way south because, of course, it was behind me.

A steady breeze blew in from the north-east; we could make four knots in the right direction. A fairly regular - and therefore comfortable - wave pattern came with the breeze; I could still drink tea without dribbling. I didn't expect it to last but it blew steadily for eight days; we sailed about seven hundred and fifty miles before it changed, I couldn't believe my luck.

We'd been on starboard tack the whole time, heeling ten degrees or so to port; goose barnacles had attached themselves above the waterline on the port topsides; how do they do that in just a few days?

Portuguese Men o' War began to appear, just a few at first, then a whole flotilla; they are so pretty: translucent pink and mauve; I wondered where they were sailing to? Some seemed to be going to windward, others lying ahull where the slightest wave knocked them onto their beam-ends; they popped back upright almost immediately – must have a good stability curve! They reminded me of a summer cruise in the Baltic one year when we sailed through a 'bloom' of jellyfish; we judged that there must have been one for every cubic meter of water for at least the first three metres below the surface. Then we tried to estimate how many cubic metres of water that might add up to in our little patch of the sea; the result was too big a number to be believable so we gave up and just marvelled at the phenomenon.

The steady breeze faltered and died. Slowly the waves subsided until the ocean was as calm and flat as I've ever seen it.

I stripped off and dived over the side - in 4000m of water. I couldn't touch the bottom.

I did take the sails down before diving in, just in case… and I swam around the boat and scrubbed off the barnacles.

It took four dives to get this shot!

I'd just dried off in the sunshine when a tern flew by. Despite the practice I'd had in the park in Rio de Janeiro my bird recognition isn't up to much, but this was definitely a tern (I think!). Back home I'd been told quite positively, by a dedicated bird watcher, that terns are not seen in mid-ocean.

Our position from my note in Cracklin' Rosie's log, just before I took my swim, was 28° 29'.5N 38° 46'.1W you can't get much 'midder' than that! It flew around the boat making that squeaking noise that terns make and stayed long enough for me to take a photo'.

We were going nowhere fast; for five days the only wind came from passing rain clouds. We motored a little and wallowed a lot; I worried about damage to the sails as we rolled and drifted slowly towards America.

I was itching too, probably from the salt left on my skin after my swim; I dug out the reliance shower again. I did all the right things: filled it with fresh water, having first calculated that I could afford to expend a few litres, hung it from the end of the boom and left it in the sun for a couple of hours. I put my hand on the black, plastic-bag reservoir: great, it was hot. I stripped off, not that there was much to strip off, and stood, naked, shampoo in hand, under the shower; I gripped the dangling shower rose and twisted. The whole pipe tore itself out of the bottom of the bag! My precious hot water gushed out of the hole and I stood there, mouth agape, shampoo in one hand, torn off piece of pipe in the other, and no whisky left either.

Nights began to get cooler, a good sign I thought. The barometer was reading 1019; when a little wind came in from the east-north-east, I thought we were on the southern edge of the 'Azores High' - until it started to veer which didn't seem right at all, but it did enable us to make sail.

It was just daylight when I took a bite from a fruity chunk of my breakfast muesli: ugh! My mouth was filled with the bitter taste of bad fruit. I began to mentally draft a letter of complaint to the manufacturers; then I checked the 'best-before' date on the packet: it was two years past. I didn't write.

The morning wasn't looking good either: the horizon was a dull red line beneath a huge, dark grey mass of clouds. I put two reefs in the main and went below to make a cup of tea.

When I climbed back into the cockpit the cloud had gone. All day the gentle breeze kept us going in the right direction, not very quickly, but we were moving.

I was re-setting the sails when a team of dolphins came rushing towards us, smiling and leaping out of the sea in line abreast, the first I'd seen since south of the Equator; I don't suppose they know which hemisphere they are in, or do they?

By midnight the air was absolutely still, the surface of the sea was as smooth as silk and dense with phosphorescence, brighter than I've ever seen it, bursting out from the bow in brilliant, white streaks and making a long, underwater trail behind the propeller as we motored slowly ahead.

Three Petrels greeted us with the morning sun and, almost immediately, we sailed into another vast fleet of Portuguese Men-o'-War; I began to count, got to sixty and gave up; there must have been thousands.

Then came a little wind again. As I was hoisting the main, I spotted spray being blown into the air some distance to port; a dark shape followed the spray, then a huge tail as a whale breached the surface.

Horta was sixty miles away when the first real wind, since well south of the Equator, came to remind me that the ocean is not always calm.

The distance was down to fifty miles when the stars began to appear that evening; I could see the lights of four other yachts all making for the same destination.

We struggled through the night, beating into a choppy sea.

Pico's lofty, volcanic peak reflected light from the rising sun, the first land I seen in thirty-five days; it wasn't long before I could see the distant shores of the neighbouring island of Faial.

Slowly we closed the coast, motoring against the increasing wind and waves that funnel through the channel between the two islands, until the pretty buildings of Horta peeped around the last headland. I rolled up the foresail, lowered the main and rigged the fenders and mooring lines as we pottered across the calm waters of the harbour.

There was at least a dozen boats tied up on the concrete quay outside the harbour office; we were welcomed alongside 'Kormorant', a big, German ketch. There was lots of joking and laughter amongst the crews on the waiting boats, we'd all come a long way to get there! It was a pleasure to be amongst fellow human beings again.

2808m 35 days

Horta

Horta, The Azores to Portsmouth, England

My 'phone had picked up a signal so the first thing I did after stepping onto dry land was call home. Then I joined a queue. There was a line of skippers with handfuls of passports and documents waiting to complete their arrival formalities; but the process didn't take long, the officials were cheerfully efficient - and all in the same building. Soon I was officially back in Europe.

The marina was crowded with yachts stopping over on their voyages: west, to The Caribbean or America, or east towards Europe; but there was enough room for my little boat.

Horta is lovely: modern enough to have a supermarket but gentle and quiet. People in the shops and offices are polite and helpful, and it wasn't long before I was invited aboard neighbouring boats for a drink and a chat. I had a long conversation and a whisky or two with the French skipper of the boat 'next door' – neither of us could speak much of the other's language but the whisky was international.

There was another 'Twister' in the harbour too: 'Pouncer'. I paid a visit and met Charlotte, owner and skipper, and Jane her crewmate. Charlotte had made up her mind, during a long illness, to do something interesting and exciting when (and if) she recovered; she'd teamed up with Jane and trialled the idea, and their partnership, on a voyage from the UK to Scandinavia and back. That worked so they sailed across The North Atlantic and spent some time cruising in The West Indies; now they were half-way on the journey home, still smiling.

I had a look at Pouncer's layout down below, it is quite different from mine; that interested Charlotte so she came round to have a look at Cracklin' Rosie. We agreed that there were good and not so good features on both boats but that it would be too much hassle to change anything.

The forecast for the next few days was not good; boats were coming in, a little weather-beaten, but none were leaving.

People with brushes and pots of paint were on their hands and knees all around the marina, painting their ships' logos on the wall, a tradition which started during the days when Horta was mostly used by whalers. Now there is a vague belief amongst sailors that it's unlucky to visit and then cast off without leaving your mark, so the practise continues. The walls are crowded with logos and names of boats: it's colourful and, here and there, quite beautiful. I walked along the quayside and found the logo of 'Luck of Argent' which I'd painted on the wall some years before when I helped my friend Ted to sail his boat from Newport, Rhode Island to Gibraltar. The wind then had been strong so we'd stayed for a few days. We hired a car and drove along narrow roads with hedges of hydrangea bushes full of beautiful, blue flowers, up to the foothills of Faial's volcano. I climbed to the rim of the crater and peered over the edge, fascinated by the sight and trying to imagine the power needed to create such a thing.

We had an amusing experience in a restaurant there too: it's called 'Canto da Doca' which is Portuguese for 'Where's the Dock?' maybe that's another Portuguese reference to sailors making their way back to their boat after an evening ashore. Anyway, the restaurant was crowded when we walked in; we were about to leave to look for somewhere quieter when a gentleman came over and introduced himself as the owner; he said that a table would be available shortly and suggested that we might like to have a drink in the bar while we waited. We agreed and he came with us; he said that his restaurant was the most popular in Horta and that all the best people came there to eat, pointing out one or two 'celebrities' as he spoke. At that point Ted disappeared to the loo, but the conversation continued and I was told that the gentleman dressed in suit and tie, sitting at a nearby table, was the Lord Mayor of Horta.

When Ted returned our host told us quietly that if we didn't like the food he'd sack the cook! That seemed a little drastic but there was no time for further explanation because at that moment our table was free. We sat down and ordered: the waiter placed a thick, wooden board in front of each of us followed by rectangular slabs of black stone placed on the boards with tongs; that the stones were hot was confirmed by the waiter telling us not to touch. The meat and fish that we'd ordered came raw on separate plates; we cooked it ourselves on the hot stones!

The restaurant was still crowded when we finished our meal and we couldn't catch a waiter's eye to order coffee. Before I could stop him Ted reached out and gently tugged the sleeve of a man in a shirt and tie who'd just moved within reach. It was the Lord Mayor who'd removed his jacket; Ted thought he was a waiter!

I remembered thinking how apt the name of the restaurant was as we meandered back to the boat. Luck of Argent was heeling in the strong wind and squashing her fenders against the pontoon, just as Cracklin' Rosie was now; people walking along the pontoons were heeling too.

I studied the synoptic charts twice a day in the internet café. As soon as it looked as if there might be period of calmer weather I got the boat ready, made another trip to the supermarket and booked out at the office.

The high clouds around Pico were tinged with orange by the morning sun and the harbour was quiet when I slipped our mooring lines but, once clear of the land, the south-east wind had us reaching along at six knots: past the southern tip of San Jorge, Graciosa island to port and only 1300 miles to go!

Towards the end of a lovely, sun-shiny day the wind strength began to increase again and a mass of dark cloud gathered to windward.

When the wind rises as daylight fades a sort of primaeval fear brings on a shiver and I hunch my shoulders.

But there's nowhere to hide so you just get on with it.

The pennant jammed when I started to pull in the third reef; it was only a 'cockle' in the rope but I had to raise the full sail, flapping and rattling in the wind, to untangle it.

All through the night dark ridges of cloud blotted out the stars. We were almost close hauled; it was difficult to rest and I couldn't make any sense of the weather pattern: I looked back at the notes I'd taken from the internet in Horta, drew diagrams in the log and wondered why, with a falling barometer, the wind came from the east. But there we were, still fairly close to The Azores, still on starboard tack and not making much progress.

By morning it was all over. No wind at all. But a visit from about twenty dolphins splashing about in the waves cheered me up.

Later I saw the dark, pointed dorsal fin and tail of a shark carving through the sea. Glad he wasn't around when I went for my swim.

Seven days out from Horta, seven hundred miles from Lands End, no wind and too far to motor. I sat and did a crossword, well, half of a crossword. Ida had put together a book of puzzles for me before I left; it was my antidote for frustration - until I got frustrated because I couldn't finish the puzzle! All the simple word games were done, I was struggling with the cryptic crossword clues.

Then I spent the next eight days struggling to make headway: setting and resetting the sails, turning the engine on and off and getting even more frustrated. The wind backed and veered, blew hard from the wrong direction then died altogether, and generally did its best to slow me down, which it did.

Two hundred miles from Lands End, nearly home, there was a sharp fall on the barometer: the wind seriously began to rise again. By the time the sun went down we were hove-to with the reefed main sheeted in hard, a scrap of foresail and the tiller lashed amidships. The wave pattern was no pattern at all; they came from every direction and life was a little uncomfortable; 'nevertheless' I thought, 'a bit of rough weather shouldn't spoil my supper'.

I boiled some rice, heated a little olive oil in a saucepan and tossed in some chopped onions; added a couple of spoonfuls of curry powder and simmered gently for a few minutes; then I spooned in baked beans and stirred for a while. I ladled the now curried beans onto the rice (didn't bother with a plate, saves washing up) and leaned back to enjoy the meal. The beans were off. There must have been a perforation in the can. They were definitely off. The supper menu was reduced to cheese and biscuits. And I still had to do the washing-up.

Slowly the sea gentled down, the wind veered around to the south-west and we sailed on through the night; 'home and dry' I thought. Ha!

At first light I changed the self-steering wind vane for the smaller one I'd made for stronger winds, because the wind was definitely growing stronger again.

By lunchtime I was beginning to get a little anxious. I'd already had two navigation-light lenses washed off by big waves – I never saw them go of course but I assumed that the sea was the culprit – and my anxiety was for the gear, particularly the mast.

I put the washboards in and locked them in position; I anchored myself to one of the 'U' bolts near the cockpit floor with a short lifeline. I knew Cracklin' Rosie wouldn't sink but the seas were getting bigger and steeper, and there was a nasty cross-pattern of waves rolling across from the south-east. Every now and again a breaker would crash against the side of the boat and wash right over the coachroof.

I jammed myself in between the mainsheet and the inside of the sprayhood. We were surfing on the crests, making at least six knots, and Lands End was only fifty miles ahead but I wasn't enjoying the ride; as each tumbling crest raced up from astern I was anxiously watching the self-steering gear working hard to keep the wind on the port quarter.

As the last of the daylight was blotted out by the scudding, grey clouds, I looked back over the towering, roaring waves and saw a very welcome sliver of red across the horizon to the west. 'Red sky at night...' the end of the cold front was approaching.

An hour later it was all over.

Cornwall appeared around coffee time the next morning. My 'phone picked up a signal and I called home, it wasn't quite as good as being there but nearly.

I called in and tied up on the visitors' pontoon in Kingswear, on the eastern side of the River Dart, opposite Dartmouth, for forty winks and a quick re-supply expedition to a little shop just outside the marina gate, to buy a tin of baked beans – I'd finally run out.

I took the opportunity of calling the Coastguard to report my return and posted the duplicate copy of form CG66, with arrival details appended, which I'd first submitted nearly three years before, then cast off for home.

A misty rain filled the air as I sailed eastwards through the night; Lyme Bay was as lonely as the ocean.

The rain hid the lights on the shore as we approached Portland to take the inshore passage around The Bill, but the sweeping beam from the lighthouse pierced the gloom and guided me safely around the rocky point. I headed in to Weymouth to sleep and spend a while tidying up the boat. Ida called to tell me not to come home before the 29th of June because there was to be a homecoming party in the marina. She then asked me to come home on the train, the 29th was still a week away!

Sitting on the train, watching the fields and trees going by felt a little strange after so long at sea, I didn't have to worry about the wind or the weather or the course we were following, I was confident that the train would take me home, and it did. We didn't tell anyone except my immediate family that I was back in Portsmouth. We snuggled up in our little house to be together for a while.

Two days before the party I went back to Weymouth and set sail again; it's really only a one day trip if you work the tides but I didn't want to be late.

The wind came from the south-west and we raced along, past Lulworth, over St Alban's ledge, where the overfalls were minimal with wind, tide and us all going in the same direction, past Anvil Point and on towards The Solent.

Ida had given me a copy of a painting of The Needles before I left to bring Rosie home; the view in the picture was from the west with the sun shining on the white cliffs, just as it was now: beautiful. But in my eagerness to get through the narrow, western entrance to The Solent before the tide turned I had too much sail up; the waves weren't that big but we were crashing through them at six knots or more. I pulled on the roller-reefing line to reduce the foresail and it wouldn't budge. I went forward to see what was wrong: tension on the line had caused it to become embedded in the loose turns on the drum and I couldn't pull it free. Bouncing up and down on my knees, I was soon soaked by the spray flying up from the bow and we were rapidly approaching the tricky bit at the entrance to The Needles Channel. I crawled back to the cockpit and let the sheet fly free; immediately the motion gentled but the foresail was flapping wildly. Back on the foredeck I cut the line and turned the drum by hand until the sail was furled away.

The mainsail carried us into the smoother waters beyond the Hurst Narrows.

A little further on I sailed into Newtown Creek and tied up to a vacant buoy, I could afford the time to sleep for a while and pick up the east-going tide when it turned.

Of course the furling line came undone quite easily. I rigged a new line and turned in.

Wind and tide carried us the last twenty miles, past all the old familiar landmarks, through the gap in the submerged barrier off Southsea beach, past the isolated danger mark and into the Langstone Harbour fairway.

Greg sailed out to meet us with flags flying and crew waving and I motored in to a wonderful reception in Southsea Marina on the 29th of June 2008, from where I'd set out two-and-a-half years before, after sailing18000 miles.

Ten Tips for Solo Sailing

1. You don't laugh when you're on your own! So take your favourite comedy recordings with you.

2. Electric self-steering gear is prone to failure. Fit wind-vane steering.

3. If you fit new equipment test it thoroughly before you go.

4. Do an electrical audit: add up the power consumption of all electrical equipment and ensure that your batteries and charging system(s) can meet the requirement with some spare capacity.

5. A large music library is highly desirable if you like music.

6. The weather will not be as described in pilot books.

7. The ability to interpret observed wind, cloud and atmospheric pressure is extremely useful: practise before you go.

8. Anything that can rattle, roll or bang will rattle, roll or bang and will ruin what little sleep you can get when you need it most: stow carefully.

9. Don't be afraid to ask for help - most people in most places are pleased to help.

10. Print or have printed lots of 'postcard pictures' of your boat on which to write 'thank-you' notes to the people who help you on your way.

Glossary of Sailing Terms Used In the Text

Aback	(Usually) A sail held against the wind deliberately or unintentionally
Abeam	At or near right angles to the centreline of the boat (far or near)
Adrift	Afloat and drifting
Aft	Towards the stern or behind the boat
Aft of	Behind something in relation to the boat's normal direction of travel
Aground	Resting on, touching, stuck on the sea bed (usually involuntarily)
Ahead	Forward of the bow
Ahull	Broadside to the waves with no sails and helm held to leeward, possibly to ride out a storm
Alongside	By the side of a ship, quay or pontoon
Amplitude	The angular distance of a celestial object from the true east or west point of the horizon at rising or setting
Anchor	A metal hook or plough-like object designed to dig into the sea bed
Anchor chain or anchor cable	The chain or rope that attaches the boat to the anchor
Anchor light	A white light displayed by a boat at anchor
Anchorage	A suitable place for a vessel to anchor
Astern	Toward the stern of, or behind a vessel

Back/Backing	Wind changing anti-clockwise e.g. SE to E
Backstay	Rigging wire from the masthead to the stern that stops the mast from falling forward
Bar	Shallows usually found at the entrances of rivers or harbours, sometimes dangerous
Barber-haul	A means of altering the angle of a sheet with another rope
Barque	A three masted ship with 'square' sails on the forward two masts only
Batten	A strip of wood or plastic which stiffens the rear edge of a sail
Beam	The width of a vessel at the widest point
Bear away	Turn a boat away from the wind
Bearing	The direction of an object, usually in degrees clockwise from North or from the bow to starboard or port
Beating	Sailing as close as possible towards the wind
Berth 1	A location in a port or harbour used specifically for mooring vessels
Berth 2	A bed on board a boat
Beaufort Scale	A scale describing wind strength
Becalmed	Unable to move due to lack of wind
Bilge	The deepest part of a boat, usually referring to the interior

Bimini	A cloth shade over the cockpit of a boat, supported by a metal frame
Block	A pulley
Blow, usually A Blow	A strong wind or storm
Boat-hook	A pole with a hook on one end
Boatswain or Bosun	The person responsible for a vessel's sails, ropes and rigging
Boom	A pole that sticks out horizontally from the mast to hold out a sail, most often the mainsail
Bow	The pointed bit at the front of the boat
Boom vang or vang or kicker (short for kicking strap)	A control that applies downward tension on a boom to control sail shape
Bowline	A knot used to make a fixed loop in a rope
Bulkhead	An upright wall, usually at right angles to the centreline, within the hull of a vessel.
Buoy (mooring)	A floating object, anchored to the seabed, to which vessels can tie up
Buoy (navigation)	A floating object of defined shape and colour which is an aid to navigation
Burgee	A small flag flown (usually) to indicate yacht-club membership
Cable 1	Large rope.
Cable 2	A measure of length or distance equivalent to 1/10 nautical mile

Capsize	When a boat heels too far and rolls over, exposing the keel
Car (sheet car)	A block (pulley) that slides on a track to adjust the angle at which a sheet pulls a sail
Careening	Tilting a ship on its side, usually when beached, to clean or repair the hull below the water line
Cast off	Remove mooring lines to leave a berth
Catamaran	A vessel with two hulls
Cats paws	Small, scattered waves caused by light winds on calm waters
Chandlery	Equipment for boats
Chandler	A person who sells chandlery
Clew	The aft, lower corner of a sail
Clew-earing	A small line which secures the corner of the mainsail to the boom
Close hauled	Sails sheeted in tight for beating to windward
Coachroof	The 'roof' over the accommodation 'downstairs'
Cockle	A sharp twist in a rope that prevents the rope from passing through an eye or a block
Cockpit	The seating and steering area towards the stern of a small vessel

Cold front	The boundary between cold and warm air often accompanied by strong wind and rain and sometimes a rapid change of wind direction
Companionway	The hatchway and steps that lead downstairs
Compass	Instrument showing the direction of the vessel in relation to north
Coordinates	In navigation the latitude and longitude of a point on the earth's surface
Courtesy flag	The national maritime flag of a foreign country in whose waters a vessel is sailing, usually flown from the starboard side as a courtesy to indicate acknowledgement of the national authority.
Cringle	A rope or metal, circular, reinforcing loop usually at the corner of a sail
Deck	The top surface of the boat – 'the roof'
Deckhead	The under-side of the deck above
Dinghy	A small boat often carried or towed by a larger vessel; usually inflatable on smaller boats.
Dodger or spray dodger	Canvas or sailcloth rigged to shield crew from spray
Dragging (the anchor)	When a vessel moves because the anchor has failed to dig into the sea bed
Draught	The depth from water level to the bottom of the keel

Drogue	A tapered canvas tube towed behind a boat to slow it down
Earing, particularly 'clew-earing'	A small line which secures the corner of the mainsail to the boom
Echo sounder	Electronic unit that measures the depth of the water
Fall off	To turn away from the wind direction
Fast	Fastened or held firmly
Fast aground	Stuck on the seabed
Fender	An air or foam filled cushion used to keep boats from banging against pontoons or each other
Ferry-glide	A technique used to cross a current by steering the boat at an angle to the current
Fine reach	A course which is close to the wind direction but not quite beating
Flange	A flat rim or collar usually to position or retain a shaft or bearing
Following sea	Wave and/or tidal movement going in the same direction as a vessel
Foot 1	The lower edge of any sail
Foot 2	The bottom of the mast
Forepeak	The foremost part of the interior of a sailing boat
Forward ('for'ard')	Towards the bow of a vessel
Fore and aft rig	Sails rigged so that they set along or near the centreline of the boat when pulled in tight

Foresail	A sail forward of the mast
Forestay	A wire from the bow to the mastheads to support the mast
Front (weather)	The boundary between two air masses
Furl	To roll or gather a sail against its mast or spar
Galley	The kitchen of a ship or boat
Genoa (or 'genny')	A large foresail which overlaps the mainmast
Gimbal	A means of keeping a device horizontal in a moving boat
Give-way vessel	The vessel which should keep out of the way where risk of collision exists
Gooseneck	The hinge-like joint where the boom is attached to the mast
GPS	Global Positioning System, a satellite based navigation system which provides position, course, speed and timing information
Great Circle	The shortest distance between two points on a sphere, in ocean navigation the sphere is planet Earth
GRP	Glass Reinforced Plastic - Fibreglass
Guy	Rope with one end attached to the outer end of (usually) a pole or the boom and the other attached to a fixture (usually) on the deck of the boat to prevent or reduce movement of the pole

Gybe	To change from one tack to the other away from the wind, with the stern of the vessel pointing towards the wind as it turns
Halyard	A rope that hoists, suspends or lowers a sail
Handy-Billy	A loose block and tackle with a hook or tail on each end, used to gain mechanical advantage when lifting or pulling
Hank	A fastener attached to the luff of a sail that attaches the sail to a stay, most often the forestay
Hanked-on	(Usually) a sail attached to a stay with hanks
Harbour	A place where vessels shelter from the weather or are moored
Harden up	Turn towards the wind; sail closer to the wind
Hatch, hatchway	A covered opening in the deck
Haven	A place where vessels may shelter from the weather
Hawse-pipe	The shaft or pipe in the side of a vessel's bow, or in Cracklin' Rosie on the foredeck, through which the anchor chain passes
Head 1	The forwardmost or uppermost portion of the ship
Head 2	The forwardmost or uppermost part of any individual item on a vessel e.g. the masthead

Head 3	The top corner of a sail
Head 4	The toilet of a vessel often referred to (incorrectly) as 'the heads'
Head up	Turn the boat towards the wind
Headsail	A sail forward of the mast
Heaving-to	Stopping a sailing vessel by setting a headsail aback and the helm in opposition to the headsail
Heel	The lean caused by the wind's force on the sails
Helm	A vessel's steering mechanism
Helmsman	A person who steers a ship
Hull	The shell and framework of a vessel
Hull-down	View of a vessel far enough away for the hull to be hidden below the horizon
Jackstays	Lines rigged along the deck from bow to stern to which a crewmember can clip his safety harness, thus allowing him to move along the deck whilst still being safely attached to the vessel.
Jetty	A man-made structure alongside which vessels can moor
Jetsam	Debris ejected from a vessel
Jib	A triangular sail at the front of a vessel

Kedge	A technique for moving a vessel by using a relatively light anchor known as a 'kedge anchor' which may be carried away from the ship in a smaller boat, dropped, and then weighed, pulling the ship forward
Keel	The central fin beneath a sailing boat which provides directional stability
Kelp	Seaweed that often grows in dense 'forests' whose upper tentacles float on the surface
Knot	A unit of speed; one nautical mile per hour
Lanyard	A rope that ties something off
Lead, Leadline	A weight attached to a line, used for sounding (measuring depth)
Leading marks	Two objects such as posts which, kept visually in line, guide a vessel along a safe route between potential dangers
Lee side	The side of a vessel sheltered from the wind
Lee shore	A shore downwind of a vessel which can be dangerous in strong winds
Leech	The trailing edge of a fore-and-aft sail
Leeward	In the direction that the wind is blowing towards
Leeway	(Usually sideways) wind-blown movement of a vessel

Mainsheet	Rope used to control the mainsail
Make fast	Tie securely
Making way	A vessel that is moving through the water is making way
Man overboard	A cry let out when a someone has fallen overboard
Marina	A docking facility for small vessels
Marlinspike	A tool used in ropework for splicing or untying knots
Mast	A vertical pole on a ship which supports sails
Mast stepping	The process of raising the mast
Masthead	The top of the mast
Mile	See nautical mile
Mole	A structure, usually of stone or concrete, used as a pier or a breakwater
Moor	To attach a boat to a mooring buoy or post or to tie up alongside a pontoon or jetty
Neaps	Neap tides, when the range between high tide and low tide is at its smallest
Oilskins or 'Oilies'	Foul weather clothing worn by sailors
On the beam	Somewhere (far or near) at right angles to the centreline of the boat

On the hard	A boat that has been hauled out onto firm, dry land is said to be on the hard
Outhaul	A line attached to the clew of a sail attached to a boom used to control the shape of a sail
Overfalls	Steep, breaking seas caused by opposing currents and wind and/or strong currents over shallows
P Bracket	A strut attached to the bottom of the boat to support the propeller shaft
Packet/ Packet boat/Packet ship	Originally, a vessel employed to carry post office mail packets; later, any regularly scheduled ship, carrying passengers
Pad-eye	A metal plate with a ring attached usually fixed to the deck of a boat
Painter	A rope attached to the bow of a dinghy, used to tow or secure the dinghy
Pilot	In navigation a book containing inshore navigation information
Pintle	A pin or bolt on which a ships rudder pivots
Pitching	The motion of a boat as the bow rises and falls
Poled out	A sail held in position by a pole usually attached to the mast at one end
Pontoon	A floating walkway or platform to facilitate mooring and boarding/disembarking

Pooped	Swamped by a high, following wave
Port	The left side of the boat when facing forward
Port tack	A sailing vessel with the wind coming towards the port side is a port tack vessel
Portuguese Man o' War	A floating, translucent jellyfish usually with trailing tentacles that sting
Preventer/gybe preventer	A control line originating at the outer end of the boom to a fixed point on a boat's deck (often a cleat) used to prevent an accidental gybe
Put her head up	Steer the boat towards the wind
Put the helm down	Push the tiller to leeward or turn the wheel to turn the boat towards the wind
Quarter - Port or Starboard	Aft and to the left or right, on the boat or further away in that direction
Radar reflector	A fixture which enhances a vessel's signature on a radar screen
Reach/Reaching	Sailing across the wind: from about 60° to about 160° from the wind direction
Red Ensign	The British national maritime flag
Reef 1	A shallow or exposed ridge, usually of rock or coral
Reef 2	A means of reducing the area of a sail to reduce the adverse effects of strong winds
Reefing pennant	A rope rigged to facilitate reefing

Rigging	The system of masts and lines on a sailing vessel
Roll	A vessel's motion rotating from side to side, about the fore-aft/longitudinal axis
Rudder	A vertical 'blade' at or beneath the aft end of a boat which can be turned to steer left or right
Running	Sailing more than 160° away from the wind; sailing directly downwind is a dead run
Running rigging	Adjustable lines used to manipulate sails, etc. to control the motion of the vessel
Safe harbour or Safe haven	A harbour or sheltered location which provides safety from bad weather
Sail	A piece of fabric attached to a vessel such that it harnesses power from the wind to drive the vessel along
Sailmaker	A craftsman who makes and repairs sails
Sailmaker's palm	A 'mitten' with a tough pad for pushing needles through sailcloth
Sail-tie	Strap or ribbon of cloth used to tie up a folded or furled sail
Separation zone	An area where maritime traffic is separated - similar to a dual carriageway on land
Mainsail	The sail behind the mast (or mainmast on a vessel with more than one mast)

Pole	A spar, sometimes a mast
Scandalize	To reduce the area and efficiency of a sail thus slowing boat speed
Scud	A name given by sailors to the lowest clouds, which are mostly observed in squally weather
Scuppers	Openings in the side of a boat at deck level to drain water overboard
Sea Anchor	A stabilizer deployed on a long line from the bow or near the bow in heavy weather to act as a brake and to keep the hull in line with the wind and perpendicular to waves. Often in the form of a parachute
Seacock	A valve in the hull of a boat to allow water to drain from or be pumped into the boat
Seaworthy	Capable of safely sailing at sea
Sextant	An instrument for determining a vessel's position by observation (usually) of heavenly bodies
Shackle	A metal link closed by a bolt or pin used to secure a rope or chain to something
Sheet	Rope attached to the clew of a sail or outer end of the boom to adjust or control the position and set of a sail
Sheet winch	A drum-shaped winch which provides mechanical advantage for hauling in a sheet
Sheeting in/out	Pulling the sail in towards the centre of the boat/letting the sail out

Ship's Bell	Striking the bell is a traditional method of marking time; ornamental on leisure craft
Shoal	An area of shallow water
Shrouds	Rigging wires from the sides of a boat which support the mast laterally
Shrouds - cap	Rigging wires from the sides of a boat to the top of the mast
Shrouds – aft, lower	Rigging wires from the side of a boat supporting the mast in a aftward direction
Shrouds - forward, lower	Rigging wires from the side of a boat supporting the mast in a forward direction
Sloop	Sailing boat with a single mast
SOG	Speed over ground, speed of the vessel relative to the Earth's solid surface
Sounding	Measure of or Measuring the depth of the water
Spar	A pole used to support various pieces of rigging and sails
Spinnaker	A large balloon-like foresail
Spring	A line rigged parallel to the side of a craft, to prevent fore-aft motion of a boat, when moored
Springs/Spring tides	Tides where the range between high tide and low tide is at its greatest
Splice	To join lines by unravelling their ends and intertwining them to form a continuous line; when complete the join is a splice

Spreader	A spar used to deflect the shrouds to better support the mast
Stanchion	A vertical post near a deck's edge that supports guard rails
Stand-on	Continue on the same course
Stand-on vessel	A vessel which should keep her course and speed where two vessels are approaching one another; the other vessel should change course
Standing Rigging	Rigging which is used to support masts and spars; not normally adjusted at sea
Starboard	The right side of the boat when facing forward
Starboard tack	A vessel sailing with the wind coming from the starboard side is a starboard tack vessel
Stay	Fixed fore and aft rigging from the top or near the top of a mast to the bow (forestay) and the stern (backstay)
Steerageway	Sufficient speed for a vessel to be steered
Stem	The forwardmost part of a vessel's hull
Stern	The (usually) blunt end at the back of a boat
Stern tube	The tube through which the propeller shaft passes
Stopper Knot	A knot tied in the end of a rope, usually to stop it passing through a hole or ring

Storm jib	A small, strong foresail for use in strong winds
Swinging the compass	Measuring the accuracy in a vessel's magnetic compass, usually by slowly turning the vessel and taking bearings on known reference points
Swinging the lead	Measuring the depth of water beneath a ship using a lead-line
Synoptic chart	Chart showing barometric pressure and frontal features
Tabernacle	A large bracket attached firmly to the deck, to which the foot of a mast is fixed
Tack 1	To turn a sailing boat (usually through about 90°) so that the wind is on the other side of the sails
Tack 2	The front bottom corner of a sail
Tack 3	A leg of the route of a sailing vessel usually when beating to windward
Tell-tale	A light piece of string, yarn, rope or plastic attached to a shroud or the surface of a sail to indicate the local wind direction or the air flow over the surface of the sail
Tiller	A lever attached to the top of the rudder post used for steering
Toe-rail	A low ridge running around the edge of the deck
Topping lift	A rope, usually from the top of the mast, that suspends a spar, often the boom

Topsides	The outer surface of the hull between the waterline and the deck
Touch and go	When a vessel touches the bottom and then 'goes' when the rising tide lifts her again
Trade winds	Winds which follow a fairly regular pattern around the oceans of the world, formerly used by commercial sailing vessels
Traffic Separation Scheme	Shipping corridors which separate incoming from outgoing vessels
Transit	In surface navigation when two charted objects are in line and the vessel is on an extension of that line.
Traveller	A block (pulley) that slides on a track to adjust the angle at which a sheet pulls a sail
True North	The direction of the geographical North Pole
Turn	A line (rope) passing behind or around an object
Under Way	(A Vessel that is) not anchored or attached to the shore
Vang	A control that applies downward tension on a boom to control sail shape
Veer/Veering	Wind changing clockwise e.g. W to NW
Waiting pontoon	A berthing facility where boats wait (usually for the tide) for access to a marina or harbour

Wake	Turbulence in the water behind a moving vessel
Warm front	The boundary between warm and cold air usually bringing rain
Wash	The waves created by a vessel, not to be confused with wake
Waterline	The line where the hull of a vessel meets the water
Way	Movement of a vessel through the water
Waypoint	A location defined by navigational coordinates, often as part of a planned route.
Weather side	The side of a vessel exposed to the wind
Whale Gusher 10	The manual bilge pump fitted to Cracklin' Rosie
Whipping	Binding the end of a rope with thin twine to prevent the rope end from fraying
White horses or whitecaps	Foam or spray on breaking wave tops
Wide berth	Ample clearance
Wind-over-tide	Tidal current and a wind in opposite directions, leading to short, breaking waves
Windward	In the direction that the wind is coming from